Train to Nowhere

Inside an Immigrant Death Investigation

Train to Nowhere

Inside an Immigrant
Death Investigation

Colleen Bradford Krantz

Colleen Bradford Krantz
9/24/11

Ice Cube Press
North Liberty, Iowa

Train to Nowhere:
Inside an Immigrant Death Investigation

ISBN 9781888160451

Library of Congress Control Number: 2010936214

Ice Cube Press, LLC (est. 1993)
205 North Front Street
North Liberty, Iowa 52317-9302
www.icecubepress.com
steve@icecubepress.com

The paper used in this publication meets the minimum requirements of the American National Standard for Information Sciences—Permanence of Paper for Printed Library Materials, ANSI Z39.48-1992

Author's Note:
I have used italics instead of quotes with some conversations described in this book. I used this approach in cases where I was relying upon someone else's memory of a comment made in the past. Since I was not present to confirm the accuracy, I treated them differently.

Cover photo used by permission of Erik Bock

Victim photos are courtesy of U.S. Immigration and Customs Enforcement. Thanks as well to the Iowa Division of Criminal Investigation for the forensic evidence photos and railcar photos.

Manufactured in Canada

Dedication:

For my parents, Jim and Mary Bradford,
and my eight siblings.

This book honors the memory of the eleven who died,
especially Byron, who was, like myself,
a farm kid from a big family.

We were the "sob sisters," Colleen and I.

We were the reporters at the *St. Louis Post-Dispatch* sent to talk with weeping mothers who had lost their children to burning buildings, gang violence, rare diseases, and other tragedies. We went to murder scenes, emergency rooms, and neighborhoods ravaged by natural disasters, all with orders to get the human side of the story, the emotions, "the touchy-feely stuff."

We were dispatched because we connected with everyday folks. We were young, in our mid-20s, often soft-spoken and sweet in the face, with eyes that occasionally watered when mothers cried over their dead boys and girls. Our physical appearances and personalities distinguished us from traits typically associated with reporters: older, detached, brash, gritty, and often haggard in body and spirit from decades of reporting on people at their worst.

It would have been a mistake to think that our abilities to put people at ease meant our reporting skills didn't measure up. We could—and do—hunt down sources, dig through documents, cut through red tape, and ask tough questions as effectively as the most hardened journalists. Colleen and I were not afraid to take down a law-breaking and/or unethical person, organization, business, or agency.

In her debut book, *Train To Nowhere: Inside an Immigrant Death Investigation*, Colleen displays her skills as an investigative reporter with heart and research. The premise stems from a news story that caught her attention while a journalist in the Midwest: *The decayed bodies of 11 undocumented immigrants found inside a roasting railcar rolling through the farm fields of America's heartland.* Colleen was haunted by the idea of what it would have been like inside the railcar.

But the story is much more than tragic fact; *Train To Nowhere* digs deep into the history and current complexities of our country's immigration policies while sensitively spotlighting the everyday people affected. From a Central American teenaged boy whose dreams of a better life died with him inside the train, to a professional smuggler—or "coyote"—who had promised to release the immigrants in the land of opportunities. There is also the big-hearted, hard-working federal bureaucrat—himself the son of immigrants—assigned to investigate what becomes the biggest case of his veteran career.

Through interviews, court records, and historical research, Colleen meticulously and passionately dissects today's immigration issues with dispassionate journalistic expertise. While her viewpoints remain masked, she makes readers care about the subject as much as she does. Her nonfiction narrative rivets like an action-packed movie, full of suspense as federal agents and victims' friends and family members unravel the mystery of the dead immigrants inside a nondescript railcar.

In today's rapidly changing media world, where deep investigation and heart are often left out of news stories in favor of "tweets", *Train To Nowhere* is a must-read.

Foreword by Kristina Sauerwein, author of the critically acclaimed *Invisible Chains* (Lyons) and former newspaper reporter for outlets such as the *Los Angeles Times*, where she shared a staff Pulitzer Prize in breaking news.

Train to Nowhere
Inside an Immigrant Death Investigation

CHAPTER ONE

Freight car GVSR 518018 looked like just another link in another train waiting on the edge of town. The standard graffiti sprawled across its faded coat of blue did little to set the railway car apart. The name of an old freight car remanufacturer, Golden West Service, dominated the side with its nondescript white block letters. Even the air that drifted up in the warm October afternoon, as B.J. Schany opened a top hatch door, hinted at nothing out of the ordinary. If anything, he caught only the dank, musty odor of spoiling field corn.

From his vantage point atop the train, Schany could see a steady stream of tractors hauling overflowing wagons of corn and soybeans to the grain elevator just west of Denison, Iowa. Cars and trucks coming and going from Denison buzzed by on U.S. Highway 30, running parallel to the nearby train tracks. It was October 14, 2002. The weather was perfect for wrapping up the harvest: clear skies and temperatures in the 60s. Eager farmers had been in the fields since morning. Schany, then a 28-year-old assistant manager at the grain elevator, had to help load a 100-car train with corn and send it on its way before day's end. The train had arrived the night before. Schany and others working at the Farm Service Coop Archer Daniels Midland grain elevator had already split the train into four sections.

Former grain elevator in Denison, Iowa, now an ethanol plant.

Schany had been striding along the train's top for the past half hour, hopping easily over each gap to reach the next railcar. He would open three hatch doors on the top of each grain hopper, a type of railcar loaded from the top and unloaded from the bottom. Schany quickly settled into a rhythm: release the lock, lift the holding bar, flip open the lid, glance inside for dirt or old grain. Release the lock, lift the bar, flip open the lid, glance inside.

The job's monotonous repetition gave Schany time to think. His mind would wander in recent days to his wife, Jill, who was nearing the end of a difficult pregnancy. She had gone into premature labor several times, and the doctors had used medicine to stop the contractions. They had hoped to get Jill to the eight-month mark, and that time was drawing near. She had an appointment today. The couple already had two boys, ages 2 and 4, and had found out—but weren't telling others yet—that this baby was a girl. As he moved along the row of cars, the biggest event Schany expected from the day was news of whether the doctor thought his little girl would wait a bit longer.

Release the lock, lift the bar, flip open the lid, glance inside.

GVSR 518018 was the second or third car Schany stepped onto as he began walking along the top of the third string of 25 cars. He opened the first hatch door, saw nothing, and moved to the middle one. In his rush to get the cars opened that afternoon, Schany easily could have missed them. The grain hopper might have been filled with corn and sent away with the rest of the train. Its hidden cargo might have been released from the bottom of the railcar along with the corn somewhere down the line.

Instead, something made Schany pause when he opened the middle compartment to look inside. Rather than moving along the railcar to the final compartment, he interrupted his rhythmic work to bend over slightly. The brief look would have been enough in most cases, but something here didn't feel right. He peered down into the dim compartment again. Something had caught his eye. He leaned closer, squinting. Something was there in the darkness. The shape of whatever it was didn't seem right for the typical overlooked pile of field corn. It was too irregular. Any small, hard kernels of corn would have spread evenly across the bottom as the train moved. Even if the corn had been wet and moldy, it wouldn't have looked quite like this. Schany concentrated on the darkness a dozen feet down. He saw an oval shape, or maybe several. The color was also wrong.

Schany blinked, straining to see more clearly, to sort out what was what. Slowly, his eyes adjusted to the darkness. The unfamiliar shapes began to take on a form, becoming something recognizable.

This is a Halloween prank, he thought, suddenly straightening up to look around for someone watching, waiting to burst into laughter at a well-executed practical joke. He and others at the elevator were known to play pranks on one another. Surely, one of his co-workers was nearby. But he was at the far end of the string of cars, well away from the office. No one was around.

Again, Schany leaned down, studying the sloped bottom of the metal container. He stared, struggling with disbelief about what he thought he saw. But he knew with certainty now: it was a skull.

No, two skulls.

There were more—perhaps many more—in the dark mass at the bottom of the compartment. Schany straightened and took a breath. Below him, bones and clothing seemed to be all that remained of a huddle of bodies. No flesh, just bones and clothes.

Schany stood, squinting in the sun, thinking of scenes from mobster movies. These bodies, he guessed, were dumped by some gun-toting gangsters from half a country away. As Schany sat atop the railcar, it never crossed his mind that eleven people—with dreams for a better life and a few dollars in their pockets—would willingly climb inside the railcar. It never crossed his mind that eleven people had visions of living the American dream, and saw this 140-degree railcar as their only ticket there—a railcar that had been locked from the outside.

As the realization grew that these were human remains, not store-bought skeletons tied to a bad joke, Schany slowly reached for the radio on his belt. He pressed the button. He chose his words carefully, knowing his voice would reach all of his co-workers.

Tom? I need you to come out here and look at something, Schany said to another manager, his voice surprisingly steady despite the fact that death hovered a dozen feet below his boots.

Can't right now. We're really busy.

I need to show you something, Schany repeated, more deliberately.

What do you need? I'm busy.

Schany paused.

You need to call the cops. I have bodies out here.

~

Alonzo Martinez Jr.'s cell phone rang as he turned his Ford F-150 pickup truck into the basement parking garage of his Omaha apartment complex. It was a little after 6:20 p.m. on October 14, 2002,

Alonzo Martinez.

which was Columbus Day. Alonzo was just getting home. Many of his co-workers at what was then the Immigration and Naturalization Service (INS) had taken advantage of the holiday granted them by the federal government, but Alonzo had spent the day at the office in west Omaha. As the head of the investigations division for the INS's Omaha district, which included the states of Nebraska and Iowa, Alonzo had plenty of work to keep him busy.

It had only been recently, after more than 25 years in immigration enforcement, that Alonzo had been thinking about retirement. His career with U.S. Border Patrol and later the Immigration and Naturalization Service had been a good one. He particularly enjoyed those first five years with Border Patrol, spent in the desert around Yuma, Arizona. Alonzo had patrolled the desert in a four-wheel drive truck every day. He grew to love the challenge of tracking people through the sandy terrain. He loved the chase. Not the capture so much, but the art of finding footprints in the sand or other subtle clues that would lead him to those attempting to enter the United States illegally. As a kid growing up in Del Rio, Texas, Alonzo had often seen Border Patrol agents, but had never had a problem with them.

Over time, Alonzo's career moved into the investigative side of immigration. The job changes—many over the years—always seemed to come with a move to another state. When Alonzo had accepted what he guessed would be his final assignment in Omaha, four years earlier, his wife decided to wait in their home state of Texas for him to retire. They had it planned: they'd spend time doting on the grandkids and enjoying some free time once they were together again.

On that particular October night, Alonzo would have grabbed food at a nearby grocery store, as he did most days. Before he could get out of his truck, his cell phone rang. It was his boss, who got right to the point.

Know anything about bodies inside a railcar?

Alonzo did not.

Nor did he know how these people—these bones found 70 miles away in a western Iowa town—would eventually affect his life. How this time, the bodies would take on identities, become more to him than just another group of undocumented immigrants who died trying to escape hard lives.

CHAPTER TWO

Byron Acevedo yanked on the cinch, tightening the saddle with an absent-mindedness bred of habit. The sun would have been rising most days as the young man climbed onto his horse and turned toward the trail. As is common for those who have spent so much time riding, Byron would have paid little obvious attention to the horse: a slight movement of the reins, a pat or soft word at other times. Otherwise, Muchacho, the mid-sized gelding with a coat of dirty white, would follow the familiar path through the cornfields and occasional stands of trees. The horse made this same trip to the milking corral each morning, with Byron astride and another horse tied behind. Both rider and horses knew the way.

Byron, his dark hair cut short, would have worn only a lightweight shirt and pants most mornings as he went about his daily chores. The temperature in southeastern Guatemala—usually hovering around

65 or 70 degrees—rarely required more. The mornings during the rainy season were typically sunny, while afternoons would bring downpours. May 2002—five months before a grain elevator worker in Iowa would make the grisly discovery—was the last full month Byron Acevedo spent carrying out this daily routine, described in detail by his family. By May, the rainy season would have started in Chiquimula, the region of Guatemala where his family farmed, just a 20-minute drive from both Honduras and El Salvador. The farm work would have begun to ease as lush vegetation returned, simplifying the feeding of the animals.

Byron Acevedo on his horse.

Byron, at 18, had made this kind of trek each morning for more than four years, spending two or three hours milking his family's twenty or so dairy cows. It was a tedious job without the modern equipment that has sped milking in other parts of the world. Milking a cow by hand required about ten minutes per cow. If each cow gave a couple gallons of milk, Byron would have hauled home forty gallons of milk in barrels strapped to the extra horse's saddle. Typically, Byron would save a gallon of milk for his parents and himself—much less than when his eight older siblings were still living at home. He took the remainder of the milk by horse to a pick-up point, where a buyer's car was loaded with milk from the Acevedos and other farmers who lived near the small Guatemalan village of Sacramento. Once a month, the driver would pay them. If the Acevedos were lucky, they would earn the equivalent of two hundred U.S. dollars a month from the milk.

Farm in Guatemala.

The money from the milk was important to Byron, but it was the crops—corn, coffee, and soybeans—along with the sale of young male calves that brought in the bulk of the $10,000 that the family's mid-size farm might generate in a year. As his father neared 70, Byron essentially took over the planting, weeding, and harvesting of the crops. Tractors were almost unheard of on the farms in the Chiquimula region. The municipality of Concepción las Minas, in which the village of Sacramento is located, owned two backhoes that were occasionally rented out for major land work. Otherwise, nearly all of the field work in the area was done by hand. Byron's father, Sixto Acevedo, sometimes hired others to help. Byron oversaw them while still doing his own work after the milking was done.

The family didn't need the milk payments to survive financially, but Byron was ambitious. This was a way to earn a little extra money for himself and his family. The financial pressure on the farm had eased over the years as Byron's older siblings went off into the world, some earning enough to send money back home. Although not wealthy, the family was better off than many others in the region. Being landowners automatically gave them some advantages. Others in Guatemala often had to accept work as they could find it, perhaps working in the fields for as little as $4 a day. The World Bank estimates that more than half of Guatemala's population fails to earn enough to rise above the country's poverty level, meaning they struggle to pay for basics like food and housing. A small but growing percentage of Guatemalans, like the Acevedos, depend on money sent home from family members who have left for the United States.

Byron's oldest brother, Eliseo Acevedo, had left for the United States twenty-five years earlier and routinely sent money home. Other siblings had also gone to the United States, though usually only temporarily. Lately, Eliseo, who lived in New York state, had been sending money to Byron whenever his youngest brother wanted something he couldn't afford on his own. First, Eliseo gave Byron money for a motorcycle. Byron bought a used Honda dirt bike and rode it around the farm for several years. Byron wanted a pickup next. Eliseo sent him the money for that, too, and found a used Toyota offered for sale. One of Byron's sisters left a second car for Byron.

Eliseo and his other siblings did this because they knew that Byron, like so many others in the area, wanted to go to the United States, or at least elsewhere in Guatemala or Central America. Facing a future of doing the same farm work day after day, Byron, at just fifteen, started talking about following his older brother to the United States. A few years later, it was still on his mind.

Still, Byron would have understood that few teens in the area were lucky enough to have two vehicles. He was generous to others in return. Anytime he saw a neighbor walking along the road, he'd pull over and offer a ride. Byron often drove to the larger nearby villages—Esquipulas, Chiquimula, or Concepción Las Minas—to cruise past the handful of shops and see his many friends throughout the area. He took karate classes for a while, and would play soccer around the yard during his free time. Some days he would walk into his family's adobe house and tell his mother, Maria Emilia Perez:

Come on. Get ready. We're going.

She would ask:

Where are we going?

I don't know. Just for a ride somewhere.

His mother would be secretly pleased that Byron, unlike many teens, wasn't embarrassed to take his mother for a drive.

Yet, even with the freedom that his car and truck offered, Byron didn't like the idea that it wasn't his money that had bought these things. Byron knew why Eliseo was anxious to keep him happy. They had talked about it many times on the phone.

You're the only one Mom and Dad have left to keep the farm going, Eliseo would tell Byron.

Byron's four sisters and three other brothers had all married and moved away from home. Their parents were no longer able to do all the daily work that the farm required. Farm workers could be hired, but doing so would drain the farm's modest income. Plus, who would look out for their parents if Bryon left?

Please stay, Eliseo would tell Byron. *I'll get you whatever you want so you don't feel like you have to leave to make money elsewhere.*

This satisfied Byron for a while. He didn't want to leave his parents alone. But, by May 2002, Byron had begun to feel the pull to explore again. He was itching for the chance to see more of the world than just a tiny corner of Central America. He wanted to point to the things he owned—whether a motorcycle or a car—and know that he had earned the money to buy them. Life had become too predictable. He wanted adventure. Eliseo must have understood these feelings.

Byron had heard the stories about Eliseo's trip to the United States. Eliseo was only sixteen—Byron was not even born yet—when he decided the family needed more income. As the eldest, Eliseo felt a responsibility toward the family. As was common for children in Guatemala, Eliseo quit school when he was twelve so he could help out more on the farm. Four years after that, in 1977, with his family still struggling to get by, Eliseo decided to leave for the United States. His parents discouraged him. He was too young to make the trip without the proper documents, they argued. But Eliseo saved his own money for the trip—about $1,200—and he told them he was going.

A friend gave him the name of a so-called "coyote" in the capital city of Guatemala who smuggled people through Mexico and into the United States. Earlier, Eliseo's friend had made his own arrangements with the coyote and had made it safely across the Guatemala-Mexico border then across the Mexico-U.S. border. Eliseo called the coyote, or smuggler, and was soon on his way. His destination was New York, where a cousin of his father was supposed to "receive" him. The first part of the trip took two weeks. Eliseo walked, rode buses and trains, and eventually reached southern California.

Eliseo Acevedo.

Things went badly for Eliseo after that. The smugglers got Eliseo to Los Angeles, but the cousin who was supposed to help him backed out when Eliseo came up a few hundred dollars short for his plane ticket to New York. This left Eliseo stranded in Los Angeles. For two days, the smugglers held Eliseo in an apartment. Since he had already paid for the first part of the trip and had no one else to call, they finally opened the door, gave him ten dollars, and let him leave. He was nearly broke and alone in an unfamiliar country where he didn't speak the language. For the next two days and nights, Eliseo wandered Los Angeles, growing tired and hungry. Desperate, he found a Mexican restaurant. Inside, he explained in Spanish what he was going through and begged the owner to give him work, if only for food and a place to stay. He knew he was dirty from his days on the streets, but he was hopeful. The owner ordered him out of the restaurant.

Dejected, Eliseo went outside and sat on the curb, wondering what he would do next. As he sat on the curb, a couple who had overheard his plea with the restaurant owner approached, asking to hear his story in more detail. They invited Eliseo to their Hollywood home, giving him clothes and food. They let him stay while he looked for help. It took about a month for a letter to reach Eliseo's parents, who had to travel to a town with a telephone to call him. Eventually, they called with the names of two acquaintances living in the Los Angeles area. One visited after receiving Eliseo's call, but offered no help. The other immediately took Eliseo under his wing, and offered to pay the Hollywood couple for their help, although they refused to take any money.

Eliseo soon found a job and a new place to live. His apartment was in a neighborhood full of drug users and dealers, but he managed to avoid being pulled into that life. He didn't use illegal drugs and didn't drink alcohol. He focused on working and earning money. Eliseo lived and worked in California for two years before another of his father's cousins in New York encouraged him to move there. In the years since, Eliseo had done well for himself. Eliseo first got a work permit, allowing him to be in the country legally, if only temporarily. Eliseo was then granted permanent resident status—his green card— through the Legal Immigration Family Equity (LIFE) Act of 2000. Eliseo had provided proof that he'd been in the United States since at least 1982, and that he was able to speak English. It helped that he also had proof he'd been paying taxes on his income.

A person with a permanent resident card, also known as a green card, can live and work in the United States on a permanent basis, but they don't have all the rights of a citizen. They are required to pay taxes. The application process can take several years, depending on the type of immigrant category and the country of birth.

There are a number of reasons for which residency is granted, ranging from employment reasons to asylum to "winning" a diversity lottery for residents from countries with low rates of immigration to the United States. Work permits can be sought for people in certain categories, such as highly-skilled technical workers. The waits can be up to nine years for some of the skilled workers, partly due to per-country quotas that can't be surpassed.

After five years (or less if the person is married to a U.S. citizen or was granted asylum), a green card holder can apply for naturalization or citizenship. By becoming a U.S. citizen, they gain the right to vote, right to be elected to public office, the ability to bring family members to the United States (permanent resident may also, but the wait can be longer), or become eligible for federal jobs.

Eventually, Eliseo became the owner of a landscaping business in a community fifty miles north of New York City. He married a woman who was also originally from Guatemala, and they had two boys. He was doing well financially.

Perhaps Byron would think, as he milked cows each morning, about all the nice things his oldest brother had been able to buy by working hard in the right place. Byron's own hard work earned him so much less. It would be easy, Byron may have thought, to tell his parents that he was going to visit his sister who lived near the Mexico-Guatemala border. He had made this trip from time to time, usually during the few periods when the farm work eased. However, this time, once near the border, he could look for someone who would help him get into and through Mexico and, eventually, into the United States.

He had been setting aside money. He should have enough to make it to the United States. He'd go work for a year or two and save a little cash before returning home. He could see New York, and experience a little of what his brother had experienced.

Other than his parents and friends, what would he leave behind? His siblings had already left, each grabbing their own chances at new lives full of adventure. Wasn't it his turn?

As he finished milking, Byron would heft the milk barrels onto a special saddle on the extra horse. Byron would have climbed onto Muchacho—the horse his brother had paid for—and turned both horses back toward his parents' home. Down the road, he could have seen the beautiful house Eliseo was building in hopes of someday returning to Guatemala.

As Byron neared his parents' home, perhaps he could smell the breakfast his mother usually prepared—coffee and tortillas.

It wasn't going to be easy, but Byron—at some point—decided that he would leave.

And it would be soon.

CHAPTER THREE

Immigration investigations supervisor Alonzo Martinez, still on his cell phone outside his Omaha apartment, listened as his boss, Omaha District Director Gerard "Jerry" Heinauer, shared what he knew about the bodies. Heinauer explained that the badly decomposed bodies had been found inside a railcar in Denison. Heinauer had received a phone call from the Mexican consul in Omaha, and wanted Alonzo to see what he could find out. The two hung up. Before Alonzo could make a call, his phone rang again. The consul, whose job was to help Mexican citizens in the United States and promote good relations between the two countries, was now calling Alonzo. A journalist had called the consul, having heard about the bodies, and the consul was looking for information from Alonzo.

I think you know what it's going to be, the man had said.

Alonzo, a native Texan, did have an idea. Bodies in or near trains weren't so uncommon in the border towns he frequented during his childhood and portions of his career. But it was a rarity in Iowa and Nebraska, states far from the border. The Crawford County Sheriff's Office, which had jurisdiction on the outskirts of Denison where the grain elevator worker had found the bodies, was treating it as any crime scene with bodies would be handled: they would wait to find out more before they made assumptions about who the deceased were.

Alonzo rarely conducted investigations any longer, but instead oversaw the agents who did. He saw his job as providing the investigators with the tools and support they needed to get their work done. Before getting the phone call, he had spent that particular day reviewing case files. Some paperwork involved arrests, while other documents were arrest warrants or deportation orders. He would check over the paperwork to make sure the names and identification numbers were repeated correctly throughout the document. He also checked the nationality of those involved since that would tell him what additional steps might be needed before someone could be returned to their home country. He typically sorted through the paperwork or calls that came from sheriff's deputies or police officers in Iowa and Nebraska. These law enforcement officers often had people in jail accused of a particular crime who were also suspected of being in the country illegally. The INS office in Omaha placed an emphasis on deporting undocumented immigrants who were also criminals.

It wasn't unusual for Alonzo to do this kind of work on holidays or weekends. The apartment where he lived in Omaha was quiet. His wife wasn't there. His two children were grown, and weren't going to be dropping in for unexpected visits since his family hadn't joined him on this latest career move in 1998. The many moves—including stops in Arizona, Texas and Idaho—had gradually worn on his wife, Griselda. A school teacher, she had grown tired of trying to keep her career intact as she followed Alonzo from state to state, their two children in tow. Alonzo couldn't bring himself to pass up the Nebraska job, though. He had worked hard during his career and thought he would enjoy the new challenge that came with the promotion. The Omaha apartment he had found was nice, but there were times when it was just too quiet. Alonzo could watch only a little television in the evenings or on weekends before he would be thinking about the work he could be getting done.

Alonzo got back on the phone that night after talking to the Mexican consul. He called the Sioux City, Iowa, INS office, the one with responsibility for the area that included Denison. Alonzo asked a supervisor there to send an agent to the scene right away. The agent, who happened to live near Denison, was in the town within an hour. Newspaper and television reporters, who had already been calling around looking for information, were equally speedy in reaching the scene. A press conference was scheduled for that evening.

Tom Hogan, Crawford County, Iowa, sheriff at the time, knew fairly quickly after the bodies were discovered around 3:30 p.m. that his department would hand the case to Iowa's Division of Criminal Investigation. There appeared to be eleven bodies, but the condition of those bodies was going to make the investigation more difficult. Crawford County had very few homicide cases. It was a simple decision for Hogan to hand this case over to the state's criminal investigators, who handled homicides more frequently as they assisted local law enforcement officers throughout the state.

But, first, Hogan made a statement for the increasingly restless media. Television stations were reporting from Denison in time for the 10 p.m. news, with dark shots of a train parked on the outskirts of town.

"If the lid is closed and not latched, you could open it from the inside. But if someone latches it, then it would be impossible to get out without help from the outside," Hogan told reporters that night as television cameras rolled.

Schany, the man who discovered the bodies, remembers wondering briefly—in the kind of insignificant misunderstanding that can happen at such moments—why Hogan first arrived at the scene in SCUBA gear. Did Hogan arrive thinking that the victims could still be saved, Schany wondered. Did he think he was going on a rescue call? What Schany didn't know was that Hogan had heard about the discovery of the bodies as he was doing a practice dive at a nearby pond. This is the kind of call you don't often get when you're the sheriff of Crawford County, with a population just under 17,000. About 7,000 of those people lived in the county seat of Denison. As sheriff in the relatively small, rural county, Hogan would have headed to the scene immediately when the call came in about multiple bodies, no matter what he was wearing. By the time he showed up on televisions across the Midwest that night, however, he had taken the time to change out of his SCUBA gear.

Denison is one of the Iowa towns that journalists, authors, or researchers frequently visit when exploring how recent Latino immigrants have changed the Midwestern state. The town's meatpacking plants helped draw immigrants to the farming community, beginning in earnest during the 1990s. The state of Iowa is 5 percent Latino. The U.S. Census Bureau estimated in 2009 that

22 percent of Crawford County residents were Latinos. Only one other of Iowa's 99 counties (Buena Vista) had such a high percentage of Latinos. As of fall 2010, Latinos accounted for just over 55 percent of the students in the Denison School District, Superintendent Mike Pardun said. Most come from California, Texas and Nebraska. This minority had become the majority in the school district.

On that night in October 2002, the town best known for being the birthplace of actress Donna Reed, of *It's a Wonderful Life* fame, was making national news. From New York to California, Americans started their Tuesday mornings hearing or reading the news that multiple bodies, now believed to be those of undocumented immigrants, were discovered inside a railcar in an Iowa town. By midnight that first day, Union Pacific, which owned the railcar, had figured out for investigators that it had entered the United States from Mexico about four months earlier.

Most people seemed to be horrified at the idea of someone dying in such a way, explained Craig Friedrichs, then chief deputy for the Crawford County Sheriff's Office. Many area residents wondered if there was some connection to the town. Could someone from Mexico have been trying to reach a relative who had moved to Denison? Why would these people let themselves be locked inside a railcar?

Others were more irritated with the idea that more people were trying to slip into the United States illegally. One Illinois woman heard the news and sat down to write a letter to the Crawford County Sheriff's Office: "This is [a] wonderful way to solve the illegal alien problem. Let's hope we find hundreds more, no, make that thousands more, freight cars full of dead spics. Maybe then these worthless criminals will stay in Mexico where they belong."

~

Friedrichs and the other officers who climbed atop the railcar, as it sat near the grain elevator, discussed how difficult the scene would be to process. How could a forensics team even get to the bodies? The only interior ladder didn't go all the way to the sloped bottom of the compartment. It would be simplest if the car could be moved to Des Moines to be near the Iowa State Medical Examiner's Office. The side could be cut open by firefighters to allow easier access to the bodies and any evidence. The railcar, however, was a crime scene and had to remain under the constant supervision of law enforcement officers until the evidence was collected. To do otherwise might hamper a future criminal trial.

As a result, Friedrichs, who had been in law enforcement more than twenty years at that point, offered to ride along as two rail workers took the car from Denison to Des Moines. The railroad supervisors who arranged the locomotive and men to take the train to Des Moines had decided to place an empty railcar—a sort of buffer car—between the engine and the railcar holding the bodies. They didn't want the rail workers to be traumatized by the idea of having so many bodies in an adjoining car. Still, it was an eerie feeling, at first, to be pulling a crime scene holding a huddled mass of bones. The 110-mile ride that night took longer than it normally would. As a special, previously unscheduled train, Friedrichs and the two-person crew had to pull onto side tracks frequently to allow other trains to pass. Friedrichs, the engineer and the brakeman talked several times during that long night about the horror those people must have endured. They talked about how it was hard to imagine what would motivate a person to accept being locked inside a railcar.

By this time, Alonzo Martinez had called Estela Biesemeyer, the INS supervisor in Des Moines, to warn her that a major crime scene and the ensuing media coverage were heading her way. In addition to the Iowa and Nebraska newspapers and television stations that normally covered the area, those based in more distant cities were also reporting the news. This eventually included the *Chicago Tribune* and *New York Times*. This kind of thing just didn't happen in the Midwest, certainly not in Iowa. In fact, immigration officials could think of only a few other U.S. immigration tragedies in recent history that had involved so many deaths. One had played out in Sierra Blanca, Texas in 1987. Border Patrol agents had discovered the bodies of 18 undocumented immigrants in a freight train that had stopped in the town, about an hour's drive southeast of El Paso. A second immigrant tragedy of similar scale took place less than a year after the bodies were found in Denison. It was May 2003, when nineteen bodies were found inside a semi-truck trailer in Victoria, Texas. They had died of heat, suffocation, and dehydration inside the sealed trailer.

Alonzo, who had spent a good part of his career in Texas and Arizona, was more familiar than most Midwesterners with tragedies involving undocumented immigrants. He had seen a lot during his career. Gabe Bustamante, another former Border Patrol agent and former police officer, explained it this way: "Nothing surprises me. It's not that you become calloused to it. You still feel for it, but you just accustom your way of thinking to the situation. Like somebody new that hasn't seen somebody's head run over, or a body part cut in half, or a body cut in half, or head missing, it's a shock to a person who hasn't seen it before. But I've seen it. After a while, you just rationalize it in your mind, 'Hey, things like this happen.'"

Alonzo was also more familiar with life in Mexico than many U.S. citizens because his own grandparents had come to the United States from Mexico. He had visited other relatives who stayed in

Mexico. Alonzo's parents, like himself, were born and raised in the United States. Alonzo grew up in a Spanish-speaking household and remembers the struggle to learn English when he started school. No one—not his parents nor the teachers—made excuses for him and he quickly picked up the language. After finishing high school and graduating from Angelo State University in San Angelo, Texas, Alonzo struggled to decide on his career path. He tried teaching briefly, but decided it wasn't for him. He still jokes that it was the hardest job he ever did. He joined the Army and eventually became a military policeman, spending roughly two years at Fort Myer, Virginia.

Alonzo Martinez in U.S. Army uniform.

Alonzo was drawn to the National Park Service, and could imagine spending years working in forests or national parks. But he hated paperwork almost as much as he loved the outdoors, and when the National Park Service wanted a pile of forms filled out as part of the application process, Alonzo simply didn't bother. Instead, he started thinking about the Border Patrol. He applied and was hired in 1977. He, his wife, Griselda, and their newborn baby moved to Yuma, Arizona. Alonzo spent his days patrolling the desert, learning the skills needed to track undocumented immigrants. He still considers those first five years of his career to be the most fun in his more than a quarter century of immigration-related work. "The fun part was the chasing, not running them down, although you did have to do that too," Alonzo said. "But we'd track them. We'd get on the line and look for tracks. You can look for tracks anywhere. It's an art, a dying art." He loved the challenge.

Griselda Martinez remembers how her husband used to come home from work so covered with sand and dust that she'd ask him to change clothes in the entry before coming farther into the house. Each evening, Alonzo would sit down and polish his dusty boots until they shined, a habit partly bred of his time with the Army. His pants would even have to be ironed before he was satisfied. By the time he left the house the next morning, he was looking crisp and polished once again.

Alonzo Martinez, late 1970s, in Border Patrol uniform.

"I still remember how two days off seemed like a long time," Alonzo said. "I couldn't wait to get back to work. I really got into this law enforcement frame of mind—not something you carry with you as a status symbol, but you just genuinely enjoyed your job. You have to really like it."

When Alonzo was hired by Border Patrol in the late 1970s, he was one of only a small number of Latinos then working for the federal agency. He remembers feeling that he had to prove himself to other Border Patrol agents and supervisors. Some even questioned whether he could be loyal to his country over his ancestral land of Mexico. Those kinds of questions never made much sense to Alonzo, who had always known the United States as his home. He'd sworn to protect and serve the United States for his job. How much clearer could he be about his allegiance? Yet, even some of the undocumented immigrants he caught hoped for some leniency when they saw "Martinez" on his name tag and heard him speak Spanish. Some—often the younger ones—would say:

You're one of us. Why can't you help us?

But Alonzo would respond:

No, I'm not like you. I'm an American citizen.

Often, if an older man was among the undocumented immigrants, he would scold the younger ones:

He's just doing his job. He's treating you fairly so just do what he says.

Alonzo remembers arresting two undocumented immigrants in a citrus grove near Yuma once, and how the two discussed his Spanish fluency as he drove them to the detention center. One was convinced that Alonzo couldn't be from the United States. How could a U.S. citizen speak Spanish so well, they wondered.

That was the world Alonzo grew up in: solidly set in one place, but constantly encountering people who were convinced he was more closely tied to another.

Alonzo believes that, over time, most people in the U.S. Border Patrol become a bit calloused to the stories of hardship they hear from undocumented immigrants. The stories, heard day after day, begin to sound the same: there's no work at home, there's a family to feed, there's no other choice. It wasn't that you stopped feeling sympathetic, Alonzo explained, but you did distance yourself emotionally to make it possible to do your job. To do otherwise, "you'd become an advocate," Alonzo said.

Alonzo never spent much time dwelling on the fact that one of his own grandmothers apparently came to the United States illegally. Alonzo's maternal grandfather came to Texas in the 1920s when he just 16. At the time, the rules were more lax. If there was a company wanting to hire you, there was normally a permit available. His grandfather, within a short time of coming to the United States, took a regular job working for a railroad in southern Texas. He brought his family along. Years later, however, Alonzo's grandfather would make a trip back to Mexico to get documents for his wife, Alonzo's grandmother, who had apparently never had them.

Latinos have been crossing the U.S.-Mexico border since our nation's earliest days. At first, no one paid much attention. A small group of watchmen tried to monitor the area on horseback beginning in 1904, but it was a difficult mission with so few. In 1900, when the U.S. population was 76 million, there were about 500,000 Latinos living here. The United States then entered an era where it has—depending on the political climate, labor needs and the economy—bounced between inviting immigrants in and trying to chase them off.

Sometimes the situations in the nations to the south have been so dire that thousands of those living through violence and poverty don't wait to be invited. Mexico was wrapped up in the Mexican Revolution from 1910 to 1920. During that time, the United States was willing to grant greater flexibility to Mexicans because of the violence they faced in their home country. And during World War I, over 75,000 Mexicans were admitted to the United States because of concerns over shortages of farm laborers.

Old Border Patrol office and patrol circa 1924.

It wasn't until 1924 that the U.S. Border Patrol was officially established to exert greater control over the U.S.-Mexico border. When the U.S. economy crashed five years later at the beginning of the Great Depression, more than half of Americans were living below the minimum subsistence level. As a result, thousands of Mexicans were deported in the 1930s. Many others left voluntarily as jobs were hard to find. In 1929, a rather prosperous year until the October stock market crash, more than 279,000 immigrants came to the

United States. Dramatically fewer immigrants—only 35,576—came two years later in 1932, a depression year, according to government statistics.

By World War II, the attitude toward Latino immigrants appeared to shift again as laborers were needed to support the war effort. The Bracero Program, begun in 1942, was a group of laws and agreements to bring temporary contract workers from Mexico. By 1945, more than 50,000 "braceros" were working in U.S. agriculture at any given time. They typically returned home with the completion of the harvest. Another 75,000 were working in the U.S. railroad system.

Alonzo's grandfather (sitting, front center) and father (center, standing) in the fields.

Alonzo's maternal grandfather was among those who worked on the railroads. This grandfather and Alonzo's U.S.-born father later spent many summers working in agriculture as seasonal migrant workers. Alonzo remembers traveling along as the men went north to work fields in Idaho in the spring, then moving on to Wisconsin to pick cherries, or to Illinois to pick tomatoes in summer. Alonzo, his siblings, and cousins would play in the fields while his father, grandfather, and uncles worked. Those long hours of back-breaking work left the adults determined that the children wouldn't end up doing the same thing. His father, who hadn't gone to school beyond fifth grade, was particularly adamant about Alonzo and his siblings getting a good education. His grandparents and parents were proud to watch as the younger generation finished high school and college, finding careers that hadn't seemed like real options for the older generation. It never seemed to bother Alonzo's parents or grandparents that he chose a job in which he often sent Mexicans back to their home country. Instead, they were proud of what he had become.

Alonzo Martinez as child, second from the left.

Alonzo points out that he wouldn't hesitate to arrest people violating U.S. law if they are from his ancestral home, or of the same race, any more than the police in Mexico would hesitate to make an arrest of a fellow Mexican. An African American police officer shouldn't hesitate to arrest another African American if that person were breaking the law. "It's not a question of race, but a question of law enforcement," Alonzo said.

Alonzo was eventually rewarded for his dedication to his Border Patrol job. He moved to the Immigration and Naturalization Service, moving up over time. Eventually, around the time he led the investigation into the deaths of the eleven in Denison, the job and immigration enforcement had started to feel too political for Alonzo's tastes. A few years later, he realized his job had stopped being fun. In 2004, he knew it was time to retire. By that time, Congress had disbanded the INS, and he was part of the U.S. Immigration and Customs Enforcement (ICE).

On the morning after the bodies were found in Denison in 2002, however, Alonzo climbed into his pickup, still on the job. He headed east on Interstate 80 through the rolling hills of western Iowa to join the team already in Des Moines.

CHAPTER FOUR

As of 1998, life seemed to be going well for Arnulfo Flores Jr. The Texan had earned the equivalent of a high school diploma after dropping out of high school, and had subsequently taken some college courses. He had served in the Army before taking a job working as part of a Union Pacific train crew. Flores was working his way up to the position of conductor. He was married and had a son. In his late 20s, the Army veteran was surrounded by friends.

Then he met Juan Fernando Licea Cedillo.

The two men had mutual friends in Harlingen, a south Texas city less than thirty miles from the U.S.-Mexico border. They met at a mutual friend's house during a barbecue. Flores, the conductor, remembers how Licea, who was younger, was entertaining and upbeat. He always had a smile on his face, was always joking around. Licea was often taking cell phone calls about something or other that had to be taken care of immediately. Flores soon understood why: Licea smuggled undocumented immigrants. The younger man ran a number of "stash houses" or "drop houses" in Harlingen. Undocumented immigrants who made it across the border, often using other smugglers with whom Licea worked, were taken to these houses to wait to be smuggled farther into the United States. Licea would make arrangements to get them to cities such as Houston.

Arnulfo Flores.

Many in the United States are unaware of a sort of second border, a series of 30-some permanent U.S. Border Patrol checkpoints (and more temporary ones) set up on major highways leaving the border region. The checkpoints are typically set up twenty-five to seventy-five miles from the border. They serve as a back-up to catch those who make it through the actual border illegally. They also act as a terrorism deterrent. Many undocumented immigrants who make it to U.S. border towns don't consider themselves "in" until they get past these interior checkpoints. Those who remain near the border have fewer job opportunities than those who make it beyond these checkpoints. Others are simply trying to pass the interior checkpoints to reach relatives already in the United States.

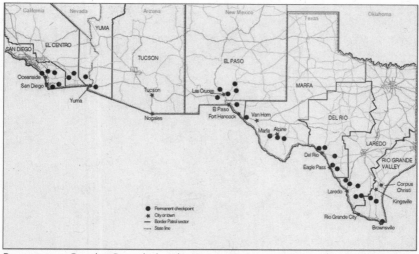

Permanent Border Patrol checkpoints. (Source: General Accounting Office).

Undocumented immigrants know or are quickly warned of the dangers of trying to pass the interior checkpoints by circling around them through the countryside. Between worrying about extreme heat, rattlesnakes, and the high-tech surveillance used by immigration officials around most of these checkpoints, other options may seem more appealing. As a result, people like Licea specialize in getting undocumented immigrants from border towns like Harlingen to major cities beyond the checkpoints, such as Houston. They are our own U.S. smugglers.

Licea, a Mexican native who was then in his mid-20s, was making good money smuggling people into the United States illegally. He received more than $162,000 between January 2001 and July 2002 via Western Union, a company often used by smugglers to receive payments from relatives of undocumented immigrants, according to court documents. This doesn't include what Licea might have received in cash or money paid through another money-transfer company.

Juan Fernando Licea Cedillo.

Licea, known around Harlingen as "Cacahuate" which is Spanish
for "peanut," started thinking after meeting Flores about how much
a Union Pacific train conductor could help build his smuggling
business. The trains were checked for undocumented immigrants
and illegal contents when crossing into the United States. They were
usually checked at least once more in the hundred miles between
there and the automobile checkpoint near the town of Sarita, Texas.
But if Licea could cram forty-some undocumented immigrants into a
couple railcars, and if they happened to get through, he could bump
his profits dramatically, especially compared to getting two or three at
a time through the automobile checkpoints. Licea didn't broach the
subject with Flores immediately, though. He waited until he felt he

could trust Flores, getting to know him better over beers at Harlingen bars or at other gatherings. When Licea felt the time was right, he explained his proposal to Flores.

The Union Pacific conductor, who had access to train schedules at work, would provide the departure times of northbound trains to Licea whenever Licea had a group he needed to move out of a stash house. Licea and other smugglers were already trying to use trains, but it involved a lot of waiting near the Harlingen rail yard since they were never entirely certain when a northbound train would head out. A large, abandoned ice factory sits on the west side of the Harlingen rail yards. It is a big, blocky building with graffiti covering the lower areas. Undocumented immigrants used to hide in a crawl space under the old building, watching the train activity and waiting to sprint and climb onto a northbound train at the last moment. Getting on too early meant risking getting caught by Union Pacific crews, who are supposed to check the trains before leaving, or by Border Patrol, which had stepped up train inspections. Licea knew that having the train schedules would make his life and the lives of those he smuggled easier since it would shorten the waiting. In return for sharing the schedules, Flores would get a cut of the profits for each person who made it beyond the interior checkpoint, roughly $50 per undocumented immigrant.

The proposal didn't shock the young Army veteran. Flores had grown up in this environment, a place where admission to the United States was essentially a black-market commodity, bought and sold by whoever wanted a piece of the action and profits. Flores was originally from the south Texas city of Kingsville, located just an hour and half drive north of Harlingen. Most people know Kingsville as being home of the historic and massive King Ranch, founded in 1853 and described as the birthplace of American ranching. For Flores, the city is home, the place he spent his childhood. Flores' father had worked in the nearby Celanese Chemical plant, one of the largest employers in the area. His mother stayed at home with Flores and his sister. Flores' ancestors had come from Spain and Mexico, but that heritage wasn't something he focused on as a child. In south Texas, Flores said, the cultures and languages of the United States and its southern neighbors blended into a sort of "Tex-Mex" environment that went beyond the food. It didn't seem to matter from what country your ancestors came.

Ice house near tracks.

Flores had dropped out of school after completing tenth grade. It just didn't seem important to him at the time. He later got his General Educational Development (GED) certificate, and earned an associate's degree in criminal law as he prepared to join the U.S. Army. By the early 1990s, he was serving in the Army infantry as part of a helicopter repair crew. He was honorably discharged late in 1997, after which he continued to serve with the U.S. Army Reserve for several years. Flores doesn't like to talk in much detail about his time in the Army. He seems to be quietly proud of his time in the Army, and doesn't want people to think his later choices are typical of Army veterans. He doesn't want to discredit the work of the other men and women who served alongside him.

After shifting to the Army Reserve, Flores heard from a cousin that the Union Pacific was hiring and that they were partial to veterans. Flores applied and was hired in 1998 as a brakeman, later moving up to the position of conductor. By this time, he had been married a half dozen years. ("I have one beautiful wife who is half Hispanic and half Italian, which makes for real bad blood—hopefully she won't see this. No, she's a good woman. She's been beside me all these years and I'm thankful for that.") The two also had a son, who was just starting grade school.

It was within a year or so that Flores met Licea and heard the proposal that Flores sell him Union Pacific's train schedules. Flores eventually agreed. Smuggling was so ingrained in the world around Flores that it was hardly a shocking idea. It seemed like so many people he knew around the border towns had some hand in smuggling in one way or another. Plus, he knew that the smugglers were already trying to use the trains to get undocumented immigrants into the country. Besides, Flores wondered, was it so bad if he simply made it little easier for the poverty-stricken people coming from Mexico and Central America to reach their goal of a new life? Flores told himself he was just trying to help. Perhaps Licea, who was in prison as this book was being written (he declined to be interviewed), saw his role in the same way. Perhaps he saw himself as a sort of saving grace.

Gabe Bustamante, then a member of a Border Patrol anti-smuggling unit in south Texas, doesn't buy the lines Flores and others used in trying to justify their actions. Flores and Licea gladly lined their pockets with the money that came from those illegally entering the United States, Bustamante pointed out. They didn't seem overly concerned when immigrants went missing, were injured, or even ended up dead, as happened in this case, he said.

Like Licea, hundreds of smugglers—or coyotes—make a living out of sneaking undocumented immigrants past U.S. authorities. Some smugglers specialize in getting people moved within the United States while others focus on moving people through Mexico or Central America. The coyotes create informal networks known as cells, loose organizations through which they hand off or even "sell" immigrants to one another as they travel north. Once they are doing enough business, the coyotes hire others to work with them, to assist in the small tasks of picking up undocumented immigrants and driving them to stash houses, or to waiting transportation, whether cars, trains, or trucks.

Rogelio Hernandez Ramos was one of those who federal authorities say sometimes handed off undocumented immigrants to Licea once he got them across the Rio Grande. Rogelio hails from the state of Aguascalientes in central Mexico. He was widely known in the village of Palo Alto, Mexico, as someone who could help people get from Mexico into the United States illegally—for the right price, of course. Rogelio had operated for many years before that summer of 2002 and, according to the *Chicago Tribune*, had been blamed by some Aguascalientes families with other deaths, whether through unfortunate carelessness or from an outright disregard for lives. Others in the village defended Rogelio to the newspaper's reporter, pointing out that anyone choosing to cross the border illegally was willingly putting their own life at risk.

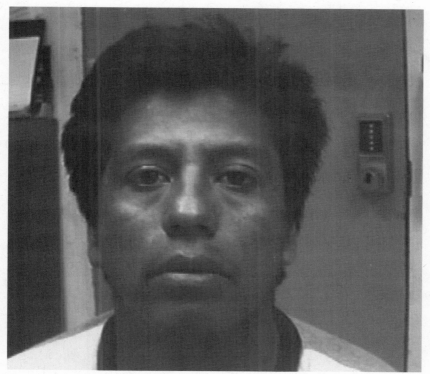

Rogelio Hernandez Ramos.

On June 9, 2002, Roberto Esparza Rico, a young man who lived in the nearby Aguascalientes village of Los Conos, Mexico, asked to borrow his stepfather's car so he could travel the three miles to Rogelio's home. Roberto, 23, and his cousin, Omar Esparza Contreras, 17, were considering making a trip to the United States and wanted to see if Rogelio could help them. Roberto was married with a toddler son. He had been gradually building a house for his family using the meager wages he earned welding, the *Chicago Tribune* reported, and was painfully aware of how much more quickly he could finish the house if he made a trip to the United States to work for a while. His younger cousin, who worked in a tortilla factory, had found out his girlfriend was pregnant and wanted to try slipping into the United States both to earn some more money for his coming child and to buy a pickup, the newspaper reported. Rogelio assured them he could help out.

Roberto Esparza Rico and Omar Esparza Contreras.

Two other men joined the cousins as they left for the United States the next day under the leadership of a man identified as being part of Rogelio's smuggling operation. The cousins were hoping to make it to Sarasota, Florida, where they would work for a while. They knew people there, including some relatives. Ten days later, the two other men who'd left with them returned alone. They had been put in a railcar by the smugglers, but were caught by Border Patrol. One of the men told Francisco Contreras, Roberto's stepfather, that he had seen Roberto being loaded into another railcar of the same train. The men didn't think Border Patrol checked the railcar that Roberto was in. But the two men couldn't tell Francisco Contreras much else.

Francisco Contreras waited another week until the end of June, and, in the painful silence, decided to retrace Roberto's steps in hopes it would lead him to the younger man or information about where he might be. He used the same associate of Rogelio's to help him cross into the United States, and ended up in a Harlingen stash house. Contreras was persistent in asking for Rogelio and finally got a chance to talk to his fellow Mexican as the two drove through Harlingen. When Francisco Contreras confronted him, Rogelio Hernandez admitted remembering Roberto, but denied knowing what had happened to the younger man. Contreras later described, in a witness statement for authorities, what happened after they stopped at a tavern:

> "I thought that Rogelio and I were going to talk some more. I saw him go to the back area of the bar and thought that he was going to come back. After a long while, I realized that he had left the bar through a back door. I saw what I thought were dangerous characters and began to get scared. I left the bar and started to walk to try and find a bus station in order to go back to my hometown. I was apprehended by the Border Patrol a short time later. I was then sent back to Mexico voluntarily..."

Contreras was back in northern Mexico by July 2 or 3. He traveled back to his hometown, having learned very little of the fates of Roberto and Omar. He wasn't ready to give up, though. He went to Rogelio Hernandez's home, also in the state of Aguascalientes, and talked to the smuggler's wife. She gave Contreras a phone number to try reaching Rogelio. Eventually, Contreras talked to Rogelio several times by phone. Rogelio ultimately claimed that he "sold" Contreras's stepson to another smuggler, a possible reference to Licea. He said this other smuggler was trying to help Rogelio get information about what might have happened to Roberto and Omar.

On October 15, the day after the Iowa grain elevator worker discovered the bones, Contreras received a phone call from his wife as he was driving a semi-trailer truck. Rogelio's associate, who had first taken the four men from Aguascalientes to the United States on Rogelio's orders, was at their home, she told her husband. The smuggler "stated to my wife that he had been sent by Rogelio to advise me that a grain hopper freight car had been found. My wife and I had already heard the news where eleven persons were found dead so we knew that this is what he was referring to," Contreras wrote in a statement for authorities. "On October 16, 2002, I received a call from a lady that identified herself as Estela Biesemeyer, and who works with immigration in the United States. She stated that she was investigating the circumstances surrounding the deaths of eleven persons that had been found in a grain hopper freight car. On October 17, 2002, I received confirmation that identification [sic] of my stepson Roberto Esparza Rico and also of Omar Esparza Contreras."

Biesemeyer, then supervisor of the Des Moines INS office, remembers the phone call. Like so many of the federal, state, and local investigators who were involved, the details of the case stuck in her memory. She got a call the first morning following the discovery of the bodies. The railcar was coming her way, she was told. Biesemeyer sent an agent to meet the train. By later that morning, the bodies had been removed from the railcar and taken to the Iowa Office of State Medical Examiner's office in Des Moines. Biesemeyer headed there with Alonzo Martinez, who had arrived from Omaha. Tents had been set up outside where the clothing and personal items were placed after being removed from the badly decomposed bodies that had been brought from the Des Moines rail yard. The day was cool and breezy, but authorities set up fans to help dry out the clothing, wet from decayed tissue. Alonzo, Biesemeyer and a third INS agent went through the clothing item by item. They pulled on sterile gloves and reached into pockets, searching for clues as to who these people were. They found some things that would help—small scraps of paper with phone numbers, identification cards, and photos of relatives. Biesemeyer took photos of the evidence. Back at her office, she magnified some of the photos on the computer to make any writing easier to read. She studied the identification cards of several men from Honduras, and found another card with the name Omar Esparza. That identification photo showed what looked like a boy, or very young man. Yet another card listed the name Roberto Esparza Rico.

The following day, Biesemeyer called a phone number that Iowa Division of Criminal Investigation agents had for a Florida woman possibly related to one of the victims. Biesemeyer reached Norma

Shoes of the deceased.

Vargas and explained why she was calling. Vargas said she had a nephew, Omar, who had been missing since June. He should have

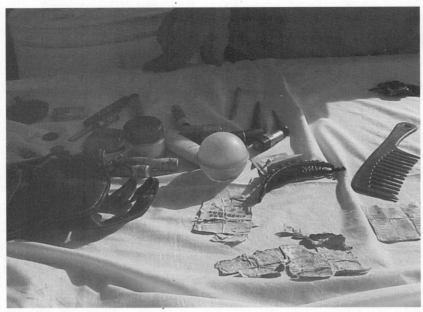

Additional evidence.

arrived much sooner, the woman told Biesemeyer. Plus, the family of Omar's cousin, Roberto, in Mexico had that visit the previous day from a smuggler's guide, who told them about the bodies on a train. The woman gave Biesemeyer a phone number for Roberto's family in Mexico, which is how Biesemeyer had ended up explaining to Contreras what he had already suspected: his stepson, Roberto, was likely one of the victims.

During this conversation, Contreras explained that after having the visit from Rogelio Hernandez's associate the previous day, the smuggler himself had just called Contreras from Sarasota, Florida, to tell Contreras that he was sorry for what had happened to his stepson, Roberto. He asked for their forgiveness. Rogelio, who came from the same area of Mexico as Contreras, also asked that the man not make trouble for him. Rogelio's associate told investigators that Rogelio tried to offer Contreras a big payment if he would keep quiet. (Contreras's own statement for authorities makes no mention of this.)

INS investigators asked Contreras to come to the border town of Brownsville, Texas, as they built a case against those who placed the eleven in the railcar. They also asked a man named Eduardo Martinez, then 21, to come to Brownsville. Eduardo Martinez (not related to Alonzo Martinez) had been one of the other men who had traveled from Aguascalientes with Roberto and Omar as they had tried to enter the United States. Eduardo Martinez, a childhood friend of Roberto and Omar from Los Conos, said, in a statement for authorities, that he had agreed to pay the smugglers $700 upon arriving in Harlingen, Texas. He was to pay another $700 once he reached Houston. He didn't make it that far since he was in the railcar that Border Patrol opened near Sarita. Eduardo Martinez had been with the two cousins when one of Rogelio's people helped them cross the Rio Grande. He described the crossing in his statement:

"We arrived in Reynosa, Tamaulipas, Mexico, on the morning of June 12, 2002, and obtained a room at a local hotel, I don't recall the name. We stayed there for one day and one night. The next morning we took a bus to a location outside of town where we disembarked and walked a short distance to the river. We joined a group of about ten other aliens waiting near the river. We crossed the river at about mid-day, using inner tubes that had been hidden in the brush. Once on the U.S. side, another man guided us to a predetermined location near a highway. We waited for about twenty minutes before a brown van arrived to pick us up. We traveled for about forty minutes before we arrived at a

mobile home in Harlingen, Texas. There was already a
large group of people waiting in this mobile home."

Eduardo Martinez recognized Rogelio Hernandez, the coyote
from his home area, a few days after arriving at the mobile home.
He heard those left in charge at the stash house referring to a person
called "Cacahuate," the nickname Licea used. Rogelio asked Eduardo
Martinez to call a relative who could wire the first $700 payment.
Once the money had arrived, Eduardo and five others—including
Omar and Roberto—were taken from the mobile home and asked to
get into a vehicle. Eduardo Martinez wrote:

> "As we left the mobile home, I asked Rogelio what
> was going on. He responded that they were taking
> us to the freight yards where we [sic] be placed in a
> railroad car. At this time I asked Rogelio how long we
> would be in the train and for him to at least give us
> some water. Rogelio responded for me not to worry
> because we would only be in the train for about one
> hour and that he would be waiting further up to let us
> out or he would have someone waiting further up to let
> us out of the railroad car."

CHAPTER FIVE

When he left his childhood home that June, Byron Acevedo didn't tell his parents he was heading for the United States. Instead, he told them he was going to visit a sister who lived near the Guatemala-Mexico border. It wasn't unusual for him to spend a week or more there. But, this time, he wouldn't even stop at his sister's house near San Marcos, Guatemala. Instead, he would continue north.

Perhaps Byron was a little sentimental as he left his hilly Guatemalan farm, thinking back on the happy hours spent playing soccer, riding his horse, or wading in the creek. Or perhaps he hurried off, his mind on the future, on the money, and adventures he would have once he reached his brother in New York. He almost certainly expected to someday return to his mother and father, his wallet fat and gifts in hand.

Investigators believe Byron walked to a nearby town, where he caught a bus to the capital city of

Guatemala, a trip that takes at least four hours. From there, he would have caught a bus to the Guatemala-Mexico border region, a trip that would take another six hours. Investigators believe he continued to the Mexican city of Tapachula.

Byron Acevedo .

Tapachula, in the southern Mexican state of Chiapas, is a hot, humid city. It's an important city for commerce, the coffee trade in particular, but is also along the land route frequently used by those trying to bring cocaine illegally from Guatemala to Mexico. However, the municipality of nearly 300,000 is best known for being the point where undocumented Central American migrants begin their journey north out of Central America.

As Byron Acevedo reached the Guatemala-Mexico border and got off a bus, he may have looked a little lost or uncertain about where to go next. Investigators believe he was approached by a coyote named Guillermo Madrigal Ballesteros, or someone working with Madrigal. Madrigal, a middle-aged man known on the streets as "Don Memo," specialized in getting Central Americans into and through Mexico. A Mexican citizen, he knew where to have people waiting and watching for more business, and Tapachula, with its steady flow of Central Americans, was a prime spot.

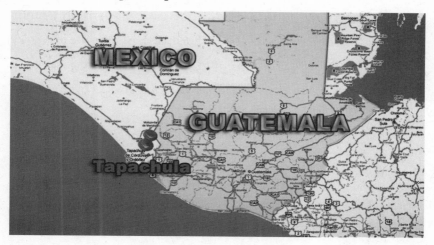

Mexico-Guatemala border region.

Around this same time, two young cousins from Honduras, Yuri and Jasmin, were on a trip similar to the one Byron Acevedo was taking. (Yuri and Jasmin, fearful of smugglers who remain at large, asked to be identified by first name only) The young women, then ages 17 and 19 respectively, were trying to make it to the United States even though they didn't have the proper documents. Yuri wanted to join her father, who was already there, and Jasmin was going to join other relatives. Their destination was the East Coast. A Guatemalan smuggler known by Jasmin's father agreed to help them make the trip to Houston, Texas, for $5,000 each. He got them through Central America and just into southern Mexico. However, the smuggler lost his confidence and somewhere near Tapachula told the two that he was having problems and would not be able to take them any farther. Instead, he took the half dozen people he was smuggling back into Guatemala. Perhaps someone who was supposed to take over in transporting the group had backed out. Or perhaps the Guatemalan smuggler got nervous as he thought about the upcoming Mexican checkpoints, usually located within 15 miles of the actual border on major highways. The checkpoints, some with machine-gun toting inspectors, can be intimidating. "And if people don't have the necessary documents to be in Mexico, it's not so much that they are going to be sent back. They have to pay a bribe and the smugglers know that," said

Cousins Yuri and Jasmin.

Alonzo Martinez, the now-retired INS investigator.

After the Guatemalan smuggler told the two Honduran women that he was bailing on the plan to take them all the way to the United States, Jasmin insisted they be given their money back. The smuggler refused, and instead took Yuri and Jasmin to a Guatemalan municipality center just across the border, where they were "sold" to a smuggler they later found out was an associate of the coyote Madrigal. That man would take them to Mexico City. Several of the people who eventually died in the train traveled with the two young women. Neither authorities nor relatives of Byron Acevedo know much about his trip to Mexico City. He may have ended up in the same group but could just as easily have traveled a few days earlier or later.

Jasmin believes crossing into Mexico from Guatemala was the most frightening and dangerous part of the entire trip. They had to cross the Suchiate River, which runs between Mexico and Guatemala, during the night. They waded and swam the river to avoid going through the Mexican immigration and customs checkpoints. Jasmin remembers climbing down a steep bank to reach the river. Roughly one hundred others were making the crossing at the same time as Jasmin and her cousin. Because of the darkness, it was difficult to see. They had no idea how deep the water was in the wide river. Most of the migrants carried their clothes to keep them dry. As they waded in, the bottom quickly dropped off. Those who were shorter had trouble keeping their heads above water. Jasmin, shorter than her younger cousin, clung to Yuri to avoid slipping under. After a short time, they made it safely across the slow-moving river.

Mexico has the same kind of problems the United States has, with its southern border being too porous for the tastes of some. Estimates vary widely on how many Central Americans illegally enter Mexico every year from Guatemala or Belize, but most place the number at more than 150,000. Others guess it's closer to 400,000. Many of those people, like Byron Acevedo and the Honduran cousins, are ultimately hoping to reach the United States.

Central Americans endure many dangers as they slip into the Mexican state of Chiapas. Those dangers include kidnappings for ransom (more than ten thousand over a six-month period, according a 2009 report by the National Human Rights Commission), rape, and even murder. Many Central Americans who make the crossing safely take jobs on mango, banana, or coffee plantations. They might be paid $4 a day to help with the harvest. Others take factory jobs that are more difficult to find at home or that simply pay better than similar jobs in Central America. Still others aren't looking for work in Mexico at all, but instead intend to make it to the United States. Regardless of where the undocumented immigrants are heading, the Mexican government tries to deport those entering illegally, but has criticized the United States for its own efforts to limit illegal immigration. The Mexican government has also demanded better treatment of its citizens who enter the United States illegally and has pushed for amnesty. Central Americans report more human rights abuses when entering Mexico illegally than when entering the United States.

A former Mexican resident named Allan Wall (www.allanwall. info) blogged about one incident in March, 2008, in the southern state of Oaxaca where Mexican immigration authorities stopped a train carrying hundreds of undocumented immigrants from Central America. Many of the migrants were beaten with sticks after they tried to flee, some until they bled. Wall wrote:

> "We must distinguish between the sort of mistreatment and abuse displayed in Oaxaca, and simply enforcing immigration law. Open borders promoters try to confuse the two. There's no reason illegal aliens can't be humanely detained and deported. In many respects, we can learn from Mexican immigration policy. To provide one example, although the Mexican government is horrified at the prospect of U.S. cops enforcing immigration law, in Mexico the police are not only allowed to enforce immigration— they are required to do so. And while we must condemn the sorts of abuses which took place in Oaxaca, I would certainly support Mexico's right to control its own

borders and manage its own immigration policy, and to detain and deport illegal aliens, as it does. But what's tiring are the constant lectures from Mexicans on how badly Mexican illegal aliens are treated in the U.S., in light of the Oaxaca incident (and many others.)"

After Jasmin and Yuri made their way into southern Mexico by wading the river, they were handed off to Madrigal's smuggling operation and loaded with 80-some others into the back of a semi-trailer truck. The immigrants were told to dress warmly because the trailer was supposed to be refrigerated. Instead, the trailer was stifling hot. It was difficult to breathe. The immigrants sat amid uncured cattle hides, which put off a horrible stench in the heat. During the drive to Mexico City, nearly everyone fainted at some point, whether from the heat or from the odor. The only bathroom was a bucket in which the immigrants had to urinate. Jasmin and Yuri avoided drinking any water during the trip because they didn't want to have to use the bucket in front of the many men in the trailer. The trip took an agonizing thirty hours. Finally, around 7 p.m. on the second night, they arrived in Mexico City. The group was given time for a shower and meal at a hotel, before leaving again around 2 a.m. This time, they traveled by bus for the remainder of the trip to the Mexico-U.S. border.

꙳

Byron Acevedo also reached Mexico City around this time. Another man brought by Madrigal to a Mexico City hotel would remember meeting Byron there on June 9. Byron, whom authorities say was also being smuggled through Mexico by Madrigal's people, likely would have made the final leg of the trip through Mexico by bus just as the Honduran cousins did.

Jasmin and Yuri were given phone numbers to call when they reached the end of their bus trip to northern Mexico. Within 20 minutes of making the call, they were picked up and taken to Reynosa, Mexico, a border town near McAllen, Texas. They joined a group of about 25 others and prepared to wade across the Rio Grande to reach the United States. As they began to cross, they heard a motor which they worried belonged to a Border Patrol boat, so the group returned to the Mexican side of the river and hid. Once all was quiet again, they successfully crossed the Rio Grande, two people per inner tube. The group waited briefly before they were picked up by smugglers and taken to stash houses in Harlingen.

In the end, the trip cost the two cousins $7,000 each and took a month and a half. They had saved some of the money in advance. Most was paid by relatives though, whom they would repay if possible with the wages they earned once inside the United States. The cost of traveling to the United States illegally has gone up since U.S. border security has increased after the September 11th terrorist attacks. Fewer people try entering the United States without the help of a smuggler. Smugglers, as a result of greater demand for their services and greater difficulty getting people past the border, are demanding higher payments. Often, a person will pay three times what they would have paid a decade ago.

Immigrant smuggling between the United States and Mexico was a $5 billion-a-year industry as of 2003, according to *Time* magazine. Although it's difficult to get exact numbers on how many people are smuggled, the *Economist* used an estimate in 2005 that more than 350,000 illegal immigrants are smuggled annually from Mexico into the United States.

On June 14, five days after Byron was seen in Mexico City, the phone rang in the New York house of his oldest brother, Eliseo Acevedo. Eliseo's wife, Norma, answered.

"*Hello*," the caller said in Spanish. "*It's Byron.*"

Norma asked her young brother-in-law how he was, to which he answered that he was fine. "*Are you sure?*" she asked.

"*Yes, I just need money,*" Byron told her.

Byron explained that he was in Texas, and needed money to pay his smugglers. Norma wrote down a phone number, promising that she would have Eliseo call back. It was the last time she would talk to Byron.

Eliseo was alarmed when his wife called him at work to say that Byron was in the country. Eliseo hurried home and called the smugglers' number, asking to speak to his brother. He wanted to make sure he was safe.

"I said, 'Byron, what are you doing!? Is it true that you are already in Brownsville?'" Eliseo remembers how Bryon told him that he was on the way to see him in New York, but had run out of money. Byron explained that he had left Guatemala a little more than a week before, which would be a relatively quick trip considering he crossed two borders and one country illegally. The 18-year-old explained that he hadn't told their parents he was coming to the United States.

"*You can call my parents and let them know that I'm okay,*" he told Eliseo.

Eliseo called their parents in Guatemala that night to tell them where Byron was. His mother, Maria, was hurt and worried. Why didn't Byron trust me enough to tell me, she wondered aloud to her oldest child. If she and her husband, Sixto, couldn't have changed their youngest son's mind, at least they would have stood behind him.

Eliseo believes that phone call represents the moment his mother's suffering began.

Byron's parents, Sixto and Maria.

At that moment, their 18-year-old son, Byron, was inside a Harlingen, Texas, stash house, waiting for the trip to Houston. For at least part of his wait he was in a brick house in a newer, middle-class neighborhood on the southwest side of the southern Texas city. More than fifty other immigrants were staying in the same house in the quiet neighborhood. The house had been rented out and the owner would remember, years later, how the house had been damaged and left a mess when the people renting left. The landlord said she had no idea it had been used as a stash house. Neighbors also noticed little, if anything, unusual during the time investigators say it was used as a stash house. This is likely due to the fact that Licea, the smuggler in charge of the Harlingen house, kept a tight lid on things, instructing those managing the houses for him to keep the undocumented immigrants inside and out of sight. A man interviewed in Mexico after the deaths told investigators how the people in charge of another of Licea's stash houses kept things quiet: "A subject identified as 'Pirana' was in charge of keeping the aliens from wandering outside the house or from arousing any suspicion. Pirana would bark out orders to a large group of aliens that filled the house. At one time he admonished [the man] for looking out a window."

One-time stash house.

Licea had taken the undocumented immigrants off the hands of several smugglers—including Rogelio and Madrigal—who worked on the Mexican side of the border. He was to handle the remainder of their trips past the U.S. checkpoints. The two young cousins from Honduras were in the same house as Byron Acevedo. Licea would stop by the house from time to time to make sure there was enough food. He would also make lists of who still remained, noting whose relatives had already paid.

Most of the undocumented immigrants didn't have permission to leave the house, but Yuri and Jasmin befriended the wife of one coyote, which gave them a greater degree of freedom. The older woman took the teenagers along with her shopping and on visits to nearby towns. One day, she took them to the beach. When they returned to the house, they were scolded by one of Licea's associates for missing a ride to the Harlingen rail yard.

"You are not tourists!" they were told.

That trip to the beach, however, may very well have saved the lives of the two teenagers. The group that left while the two were at the beach included some of the eleven who ultimately died inside the railcar. Yuri and Jasmin, who were later able to get temporary documents to remain in the United States so they could act as witnesses if a criminal trial were held, are aware how lucky they were to have missed the train that day. They started to laugh about their crazy luck, but they knew some of the victims. They became serious when they talked about them. They knew sisters Lely Elizabet Ferrufino and Rosibel Ferrufino, and their niece Lesly "Esmeralda" Ferrufino, who lived near one of the cousins' homes in Honduras. They got to know others during the trip from Central America, including Pedro Amador Lopez, 37, also from Honduras, and Mercedes Gertrudis Guido Lorente, 40, who was from Nicaragua and appeared to be acting as a guide for smuggler Madrigal during part of the trip. The two cousins' own uncle, who had traveled with them earlier in the journey, was loaded on the same train, but ended up in a different railcar than the victims.

In the days and weeks after the group was loaded into the train, Yuri, Jasmin, and their U.S. relatives got desperate phone calls from relatives of the three Ferrufino women. The Ferrufinos' relatives were calling them, knowing they had traveled together in Central America. The young cousins, however, couldn't give them much helpful information.

They couldn't give them what they wanted most: hope.

CHAPTER SIX

The area around Harlingen, Texas, is, in large part, a mix of retired northerners looking to escape blizzards and ice storms, native Texans whose families have lived in the area for generations, and recent immigrants looking for a way to make a little more money in the border region or beyond.

As of 2010, the city's population was over 64,800. While the U.S. Census Bureau has become more determined to count all people—including those residing illegally—this number may not include many undocumented immigrants who would not want to be found. Almost three-quarters of Harlingen's residents categorize themselves Latino or "Hispanic." Nationally, Latinos account for 15 percent of the population. Only 19 percent of Harlingen's residents ages 25 and older had earned at least a Bachelor's degree, compared to the estimated national average of just over 27 percent. Harlingen had an estimated median household income of around $35,000, while the median household income for the United States was just over $52,000.

The Harlingen Convention and Visitors Bureau tells potential visitors about a variety of things to do, including a nature trail "where parrots and sub-tropical birds rule," Mexican bakeries featured in *Southern Living,* and the Blues on the Hill concerts. The city is also just a short distance from South Padre Island or from "cold margarita drinks in old Mexico." Another local industry isn't mentioned, however; the smuggling of Mexicans and Central Americans. Many visitors passing through the town might not be fully aware of what goes on since the action tends to be much more subtle than what tourists may see in true border towns, such as swimmers trying to cross the Rio Grande. As in many towns in the Lower Rio Grande Valley, thousands of dollars trade hand, from would-be immigrants to smugglers.

The desperation of the undocumented immigrants feels commonplace to area residents, and their deaths can be treated with an almost-casual attitude bred of familiarity. More than once, Harlingen-area residents asked why the railcar deaths of the eleven would be considered a story worth retelling. "It happens all the time," one person said. Usually, they would back off a bit and acknowledge that fewer people were usually involved in single incidents. Still, they would point out, people often drowned in the Rio Grande or on cross-country attempts to reach the interior of the United States.

Until at least the late 1990s, residents of The Valley would frequently see undocumented immigrants climbing into standing railcars, or running and jumping on as a northbound train began to pull away. "You'd watch a train go by and you could see people on there, hanging off the sides of the cars," said Flores, the former Union Pacific conductor.

Border Patrol inspections of freight trains in the so-called McAllen Sector of Texas—which includes Harlingen, Corpus Christi, Brownsville, McAllen, and Kingsville—resulted in the arrests of more than 11,000 undocumented immigrants in fiscal year 1997. Around this time, state and federal officials in Texas boosted enforcement efforts through a program called "Operation Rio Grande," which they credit with a subsequent decrease in the number of undocumented immigrants arrested on area trains. By 1999, two years later, the number of arrests had been cut by more than half, with 4,692 arrested. The numbers continued a general downward trend, with just 257 arrests in fiscal year 2009, according to the Border Patrol. These numbers could, in theory, suggest to skeptics that the Border Patrol is missing more people on the trains and simply making fewer arrests as a result. Flores, the former train conductor, however, believes the same thing that the Border Patrol appears to believe: that the inspections did get tougher and were more effective. Flores, who was on trains through that area regularly for his job, noticed a difference over time. Many smugglers and undocumented immigrants looked for other ways to slip beyond the interior checkpoints. It's likely that a combination of factors—such as Operation Rio Grande's increased surveillance, the gradual increase in Border Patrol agents over time (not just after Sept. 11, although the states bordering Mexico did see an overall increase of almost 800 Border Patrol agents from 2001 to 2005), and the media attention paid to the deaths of the eleven—worked together to account for the dramatic decline in train arrests in The Valley between 1997 and 2009.

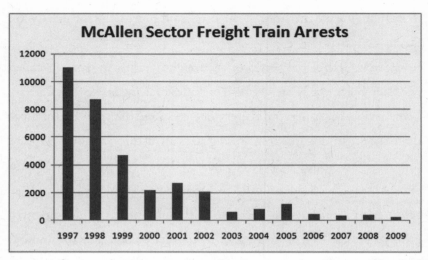

McAllen Sector Freight Train Arrests

As of 2002, though, one smuggler in particular, Licea, still relied heavily upon trains as he tried to slip undocumented immigrants northeast to Houston and beyond. The fact that he had reached an agreement with Flores, who could provide train schedules, made using the trains much easier. Before that, smugglers and their customers had to wait around near the tracks for long stretches at a time, waiting for a northbound train to move out. With the schedules in hand, the waits became shorter, and Licea became known as the guy with someone on the "inside."

In Harlingen, the railroad tracks run right through the heart of the city. The rail yard is pinched between a busy commercial neighborhood and a quiet, largely residential neighborhood, which is where undocumented immigrants would often try to slip in. The old abandoned ice factory was a common spot where undocumented immigrants would wait. Often, while doing his required train inspections as a part of a Union Pacific crew, Flores would notice how items such as clothes or old handbags had been left behind in the large crawl space under the massive building, presumably abandoned by undocumented immigrants sprinting or sneaking quietly toward a train. The Ice House was accessible through the residential neighborhood, and more than a hundred people could easily hide beneath the building without being seen, though typically groups would be much smaller.

On the night of June 15, 2002, however, the majority of the undocumented immigrants who were loaded onto a northbound train didn't have to wait beneath the Ice House. Eduardo Martinez, the man from Mexico who had asked for—but didn't receive—water before entering a second railcar, described in a statement for immigration officials what he and his friends from Mexico, cousins Roberto Esparza Rico and Omar Esparza Contreras, saw. He described how about 25 others were waiting to be loaded onto the train when his own group reached the Harlingen rail yard that night. Byron Acevedo, the young man who had traveled so far from his parents' Guatemalan farm, would have been in the group. Several "guides" appeared to be coordinating things at the rail yard for the smugglers. Eduardo Martinez wrote:

> "The guides told us to form a single file and we walked a few minutes to the train we were to be loaded into. The guides loaded about half the group into a "tolba" (grain hopper car) that was next to the last car in the train. It appeared they wanted to keep the group close together so they just went to the next car and loaded several of the aliens into it too. At this time, the second hopper car also appeared to be full and they (guides) noticed there was [sic] still four of us left: myself, Roberto, Omar, and another person I know as "Guero." The guides told us to go two each into the separate hopper cars."

It was this small twist of fate—the dividing of a few remaining men among two railcars—that ultimately saved Eduardo Martinez's life, but not those of Roberto and Omar, who ended up in the ill-fated railcar.

Eduardo Martinez mentions noticing only one person inside his railcar who grew nervous enough about the idea of riding inside a hot and dusty grain hopper to get out at the last moment:

"It appeared that two guides joined us at this time,
one in each hopper car. When the train started to move,
the guide traveling with my group said he was scared
and left. He appeared to be a very young boy."

It is not uncommon for teenage boys to be used as guides who serve as low-level assistants to coyotes such as Licea. The boys would be paid to ride along with the group to ensure they reached the next destination safely. Many of these boys were undocumented immigrants themselves. They worried about getting caught and sent back home. Such boys tend to start this type of work out of desperation, but often stay with it when they begin to move up the ranks. Eventually, it seems safe to reason, going off to start their own smuggling operation.

Manuel Alexis Funez, a Honduran man who was also in the railcar abandoned by the young guide, said he believed that one of the victims, Mercedes Gertrudis Guido Lorente, 40, from Nicaragua, may have been acting as a guide for another smuggler, Guillermo Madrigal. Mercedes had led Manuel Funez and his nieces, the two young women who missed the ride in the railcar because of the trip to the beach, from Mexico City to the U.S. border. It's possible Mercedes may have simply been a passenger by the time the group was handed off to Licea's network. Or perhaps she had a deal where she traveled for a discount or for free. Mercedes had two grown children in Nicaragua, a son and daughter. She'd had little contact with them in the preceding years, however, as she traveled throughout Central America and Mexico. An FBI special agent who interviewed her relatives said the children heard from her only occasionally. "It was like she just kind of did her own thing," the FBI's Rosemary Amerena said. "Her children said, 'Sometimes we see her, and sometimes we don't.'"

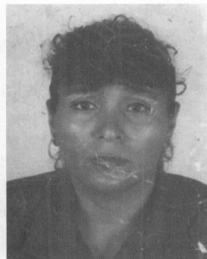

Guillermo Madrigal Ballesteros (Don Memo) and Mercedes Gertrudis Guido Lorente (victim).

Investigators believe a young man was riding on the outside of the grain hopper that Mercedes and the ten others were in, but abandoned the car as the other young guide had, although not until the train was stopped for the Border Patrol inspection.

When Byron Acevedo climbed into that grain hopper after more than a week of traveling, he must have felt like he was so close to his dream and his new life in the United States, a place he'd heard of all his life as the place you went to make real money.

The grain hoppers wouldn't have been the most pleasant traveling vessels in any occasion. But in the southern Texas June heat, it would have been uncomfortable almost immediately. Those climbing inside from the top would have climbed down a short ladder and then dropped to the sloped bottom. They would have found a spot to sit in the crowded compartment. Once the top hatch door was closed and latched by the guides, or others working with the smugglers, the heat and humidity would have worsened.

Metal latch on hopper door.

No one will ever know what the mood was like inside that grain hopper as the train lurched forward the first time and began to move. Was there a quiet nervousness? Or did the group give a small cheer as the train started moving? Did anyone have second thoughts at the last minute and try unsuccessfully to get out?

Those who survived their own trip after being caught by Border Patrol can tell us what it was like in their railcar. Manuel Funez, from Honduras, wrote in his statement: "It was very dusty inside the railroad car. ... Every time the train moved the air got worse, and it was very hard to breathe. I believe we would have died in the railroad car if Immigration had not caught us."

The guides had closed and locked the metal latch on the top hatch door to avoid drawing the attention of Border Patrol during any possible inspection. Typically, the guides working for the smugglers would open the hatch door when the occupants successfully made it beyond the Border Patrol checkpoint. They were to be released at the next point when the train stopped for more than a minute or two. Often, for this network of smugglers, this would have been in or near Kingsville, Texas, an hour-and-a-half drive by car from Harlingen. The smugglers would then have taken them in cars and trucks to Houston, where the undocumented immigrants would make their own arrangements to reach other parts of the United States if they were continuing on.

Union Pacific track records, collected by the San Antonio law firm, Prichard, Hawkins, McFarland & Young, show that the train left Harlingen shortly after 10 p.m. on June 15. Records indicate the train was inspected about three hours later by Border Patrol. One of the men who survived the ride, however, estimated that the train had only been moving for perhaps an hour. Eduardo Martinez described the ride: "During that hour, it was very hot in the hopper car and it appeared water drops were falling from the roof. It may have been because of the heat inside and the heat from our bodies inside the car."

As the train came to a stop somewhere near the unincorporated Kenedy County town of Armstrong, fifty-four miles north of Harlingen, those inside would have waited. Perhaps they whispered, fearful of being discovered and having to repeat the journey all over again. They might have discussed why and where they were stopped.

Had they reached Kingsville? Were the coyotes' associates about to open the top door? Was it a Border Patrol inspection stop?

Some, particularly those suffering the most from the heat and lack of ventilation, might have been secretly hoping to be discovered. Some may have even considered calling out. In the end, they likely decided they were too close to reaching their destination to blow it by letting a little heat get to them. They might not have wanted to anger the others. It was best to remain quiet and just wait. It would be over soon, they hoped.

The guide might open the door any minute.

CHAPTER SEVEN

The railway cars' rattling halted as the train came to a stop that night. The resulting quiet more than likely was unnerving to some of the 37 people hiding inside the two railcars. It was around 1 a.m. on June 16. At least an hour had passed—perhaps as many as three—since they had climbed inside the railcars. Either way, it would have felt like a long time to those inside, due to the intense heat and humidity.

The men and women might not have realized it yet, but the train had stopped for an inspection by the U.S. Border Patrol. Typically, the agents rotate the location at which they conduct train inspections from day to day. The Border Patrol has a small building along U.S. Highway 77 near Sarita, Texas, the next town north of Armstrong. Cars and trucks traveling the highway must stop for a few quick questions or, if an agent so decides, for a full inspection. The rail line in this area runs parallel to Highway 77, which would make it easy for agents to conduct train inspections right next to the Sarita automobile inspection building. They instead tend to conduct the train inspections at random locations, stopping trains at a variety of spots along the 70-some miles of track separating Harlingen and Sarita. The strategy makes it more difficult for smugglers to decide where to load and unload undocumented immigrants.

On this particular night, the train was stopped near Armstrong, 20 miles south of Sarita. The Border Patrol declined to release its documents related to this incident as of the publishing of this book, citing the open criminal case against two smugglers as the reason for the refusal. Between documents from other federal agencies and numerous interviews, a relatively clear picture of how things played out that night begins to emerge.

The stop near Armstrong wasn't what the smugglers had wanted. The coyotes' goal had been to get the undocumented immigrants past Sarita. They had planned to unlock the top compartment doors, releasing the two carloads of people when the train pulled over to let another train pass at some point beyond Sarita, perhaps in Kingsville.

The Border Patrol agents near Armstrong that night had dogs that were trained to search for hidden passengers. The agents, at least one with a dog, would typically walk the length of the train to check for trespassers. If it had been a still night, the dog would have picked up the immigrants' scent as it walked close to an occupied railcar. With any breeze at all, the scent might have been carried on the wind toward the dog. Border Patrol inspectors, knowing they had someone in one of the railcars, would have taken over the search to pinpoint exactly where people were hiding.

Agents sometimes pound the lower side of an empty grain hopper, knowing that it would sound differently when full of people rather than sitting empty. Agents using flashlights during night-time inspections sometimes walk along the top of grain hoppers, opening and looking inside any with unlatched doors.

Eduardo Martinez, one of the undocumented immigrants who survived the trip, wrote what happened that night:

> "After a while, we heard Immigration checking the car next to us. Immigration opened the door to the hopper car we were in and shined the light on us. Someone in our group told him to let us out because it was very hot. The Immigration Officer told us to wait while he checked the next car and closed the door. I heard him checking the next car and he came back after about two minutes."

Some of the undocumented immigrants who were caught that night described the two occupied railcars as being next to one another. It appears from witness descriptions that Border Patrol agents at least superficially checked both adjoining railcars, but the second group was overlooked somehow. The officer may have only looked in one of the three separate compartments in the railcar. The group of eleven sat in the middle compartment.

"So they probably got the first group and you reward the dog," said Alonzo Martinez, the now-retired investigator who helped interview the Border Patrol agents who were there that night. "The dog probably thinks it has done its job. And it's probably tired and hot. And with all those people now outside from the first car, the scent is everywhere so the dog never alerts again."

The inspectors officially inspected the entire train, but relied upon the dogs to help them do so. And, like the dogs, perhaps they were tired and hot and distracted by the big group of twenty-six found in the first railcar. "Nothing takes the place of inspecting every nook and cranny, but these agents were dealing with the first group and had to get them taken off," Alonzo Martinez said.

The closed latch handle may have done exactly what the smugglers had intended: the agents may have been less concerned with the second railcar because it was locked.

Early in his career, Alonzo Martinez worked as a Border Patrol agent and saw first-hand how the job hardens some people. The agents hear so many stories of hardships that eventually they all begin to sound the same, and they tire of hearing them. But even some of those calloused by the thankless job would likely have had some regrets to later find out they had missed a chance to save eleven lives. Perhaps as much as anything, they might have worried about what consequences they would face on the job as a result of those eleven making it through their inspection. The September 11th attacks were not yet a year in the past when the train passed from Mexico into Texas. The bosses in

Washington D.C. were demanding tighter borders and there was a good chance of an uproar—at least internally—if there were major failures, especially one playing so prominently in the media.

By the time the train reached the surprise inspection site near Armstrong, the conditions inside the freight cars were harsh. When the Border Patrol emptied out the first railcar, some of the twenty-six inside were already showing symptoms of dehydration and heat stroke. One woman taken off was crying and panicking. She was feeling faint, and had to be treated for dehydration. This all took place during the night.

Of course, no one knows for certain whether things might have been better or worse in the second railcar that held the eleven. But the cars were not far from one another and were both grain hoppers. If the people inside drank similar amounts of water before getting inside the railcars, and considering that they were all young to middle-age adults, it's likely their conditions were worsening at roughly the same pace. It's also probably a safe assumption that when the Border Patrol dogs began sniffing around a few cars down, the eleven were keeping quiet inside their own grain hopper despite their discomfort, hoping to avoid being caught. Neither the Border Patrol agents interviewed by investigators, nor those taken off the other grain hopper ever mentioned hearing anything from the car carrying the eleven.

Undocumented immigrants taken from the first car by Border Patrol agents would later talk about what it had been like inside. When they first got into the car, they could actually see steam rising. Gradually, water began to drip from the ceiling of the closed compartment as the moisture from their bodies condensed on the underside of the lid. It was almost like it was raining inside. If they hadn't already been soaked with their own sweat, these falling drops would have done the job. With every breath, moisture was being added to the already humid conditions. Sweat poured from them. And, if anyone had to urinate, that was another bit of moisture in the close quarters.

"The humidity outside would have been nothing compared to inside," said Mark Blumberg, author of *Body Heat: Temperature and Life on Earth*. "It was like they were in a humidor."

The human body regulates its own temperature within a range of a few degrees, roughly from 97 to 99 degrees Fahrenheit. If the air temperature is cooler than 97 degrees, but a person's body is warming from exercise or for some other reason, humans can radiate heat to their surroundings to keep the body's temperature in the correct range. When things heat up in the outside world to a point above 99 degrees, however, the human body has just one way to cool itself, according to Blumberg, University of Iowa psychology professor: it sweats. On June 15 and 16, 2002, the temperature in nearby Brownsville, Texas, climbed to a high of 96 degrees. The low at night was in the mid- to high-70s. But inside a freight car filled with people and lacking in ventilation, the temperature would have been significantly higher than 76 or 96 degrees. No one knows exactly what temperature the railcar's interior reached that day, but it is likely that it climbed beyond 120 degrees. San Francisco State University's Department of Geosciences once conducted a study about temperature in an enclosed space using an automobile. It showed that even with a window open an inch-and-a-half, the temperature inside the vehicle rose from the low 90s to above 125 degrees within a half hour. Whether the temperature was 120 or 150 degrees in the railcar is largely irrelevant, however. At either temperature, the dangers would have been the same.

Although those inside would have been dripping sweat, it would have been for nothing. For sweat to be effective, it has to evaporate. But sweat won't evaporate if the humidity is too high. It just drips off a person's body with no positive results. That person has just lost more water but gained nothing. The same thing happens on a hot, humid day to a person walking down the street. The sweat that drips off their body does them no good. Even worse, besides losing crucial water, the body also uses up energy and depletes important minerals.

These factors, combined with the intense heat, would have quickly pushed the railcar occupants into greater danger. The human body will battle these kinds of outside conditions for a while, but, eventually, a person has to move to a less humid, cooler place or face dire consequences. With the hatch door locked from the outside, though, the eleven had no choice but to stay put once the Border Patrol agents had left. The surrounding area is quiet and rural. A few scattered ranch houses may have been nearby, but little else sat amid the fields of tall, waving grass. Cars may have been passing on the parallel highway, but would have been traveling too quickly—most with windows closed—for the drivers to overhear any cries. They had no choice but to wait for the train to continue on to Kingsville, no choice but to hope the coyotes would indeed come unlock the door as planned.

What they didn't know was that the coyotes had abandoned the train as soon as the first carload of people was taken into custody. "The coyotes had assumed," Alonzo Martinez said, "that the eleven men and women had been caught by Border Patrol along with the first carload." The guide riding on the outside of one railcar had been prepared to release those inside once they were past the automobile checkpoint, but when the train stopped unexpectedly and the Border

Patrol showed up, the guide jumped down and fled, investigators believe. If the guide was in the United States illegally, he would have been worried about being deported or jailed.

Still, the coyotes had a backup for the guide. They had one or more of their people traveling by car along Highway 77, keeping an eye on the train's progress. Some nights, a car would sit waiting for the train in Raymondville, south of Armstrong. When it passed, they would follow. A man inside the pursuing car that particular night saw that the train had been stopped and was being inspected. He called to report this to the others back in Harlingen, then continued to drive past on the divided highway, turning around and returning several times to see what was happening. After seeing Border Patrol unloading a railcar, he called the coyotes in Harlingen to report that the people had been caught. He then left, worried about drawing attention by hanging around too long. The person or people in the car assumed—incorrectly, it turned out—that the second car had been emptied along with the first.

Perhaps, when the train began moving again around 3 a.m., the eleven inside the second car would have felt some excitement, at least a small surge of hope despite their extreme discomfort. They might have thought that they were going to make it to their relatives or to new jobs after all.

They had, it seemed, gotten through.

Alonzo Martinez interviewed some of those from the first railcar later and asked why they didn't tell the Border Patrol inspectors that a second group was hiding in another railcar. "They said they didn't want to rat out the others," Alonzo Martinez said. "They thought the others had been lucky enough to make it."

"One told me later, 'I guess we were the lucky ones by getting caught.'"

Eduardo Martinez, taken out of the first railcar, said in a statement:

> "After we were out of the hopper car and on the ground, I noticed that the other group that Roberto and Omar had joined had not been found by Immigration. I did not say anything because I was hoping that they would succeed in making their trip north. The last time I saw Roberto and Omar was at the train yards in Harlingen when they boarded the grain hopper car."

Chapter Eight

At some point, Byron Acevedo would have begun to ache. In the sweltering heat and humidity of the grain hopper, his body would have been rapidly losing water. The 18-year-old's clothes would have been drenched with sweat. He would have been battling a severe headache, vomiting, and probably feeling dizzy. The ten others packed in around him would have been in agony also, enduring similar symptoms of heat stroke.

Heat stroke is one cause of hyperthermia—a high body temperature as a result of the body absorbing or producing more heat than it can dissipate. Hyperthermia occurs when the body can no longer regulate its own temperature. The related symptoms can vary from one person to another in timing and initial severity. Factors such as age, water consumption, and being in good shape are key to how well a person initially handles the stress of heat, said Kevin Kregel, a University of Iowa integrative physiology professor who has spent more than two decades studying heat stroke and other body stressors. Those among the seven men and four women in the train who drank more water beforehand would have been better off initially, as would those who were in better physical shape. The youngest (very young children would have been the exception, but none were present) would have also, albeit briefly, been at an advantage. As people age, their tolerance for heat declines and the body is less efficient in regulating its temperature, Kregel pointed out. Other conditions associated with aging, such as heart issues and high blood pressure, also contribute to lower tolerance of extreme heat and humidity.

Water leaves the human body at an astonishing rate in settings such as the railcar, with its high temperatures, high humidity and limited ventilation. A person can produce a liter and a half of sweat per hour during vigorous exercise or in an overheated environment. That's about forty-nine ounces. "Imagine losing the equivalent of four soda cans of water each hour as your body pours moisture to the surface of your skin in a fruitless attempt to cool itself," Kregel said. It doesn't take long before a person's body begins to run out of water.

When a person overheats, one of the body's first responses is to shift blood to the extremities, the opposite of what happens in extremely cold temperatures, where the blood is kept closer to the body's core to protect the most vital organs. Faced with high temperatures, the body moves blood outward to the arms, legs, and surface of the skin. The blood vessels nearest the skin dilate, and ideally, they radiate heat off the body into the surrounding environment. When the outside temperature is higher than a person's body temperature, however, the body heat will not radiate away. It can only move from an area of higher concentration to lower concentration, but not the opposite as would be required in this case. Instead, with no escape from the heat, the body temperatures of the eleven would have begun to creep up.

Unless something changed quickly and dramatically, the body temperatures of the seven men and four women would have continued to rise. The climb would not stop until their body temperatures matched the temperature of the surrounding environment. Once the sun had risen, the temperature inside the metal freight car would have reached at least 120 degrees Fahrenheit, perhaps as high as 150. Heat stroke occurs when the core body temperature reaches 104 degrees, with a core body temperature of 107 degrees being considered fatal.

Humans have little, if any, ability to self-regulate their brain temperature separately from their body temperature. Dogs pant to regulate their temperature. They have a unique circulation pattern in their necks to help radiate heat from their blood before it reaches their brains, Kregel said. This helps keep the temperature of their brains a degree or so lower than the temperature in the body core. In humans, brain temperature will match the core body temperature or vary by no more than a few tenths of a degree.

The human brain is more sensitive to temperature than the rest of the body. It shows the effects of high temperature at a point about two degrees earlier than the body. The brain, around 102 degrees, begins to lose some of its ability to function. This explains why a child might be "out of it" when running a 102-degree fever. Once a person in a hot place reaches a brain temperature of 106 degrees, they face the risk of permanent brain damage. Beyond 107 degrees, a person has little or no hope of surviving. "It's like boiling an egg. You put that protein in water and the egg white solidifies. You can't un-boil it," said Mark Blumberg. "It's like that with the brain. The damage is irreversible."

Inside the railcar, then, the temperatures of the eleven continued to climb. As their brains overheated, a resulting mental shift would have taken place inside the locked compartment. If they had remained silent before to avoid detection by Border Patrol, this would no longer be the case. Panic would have set in, with some, if not all, growing desperate to escape the breathless, humid torture chamber. They would have flailed about, hunting for any weakness in the railcar.

Blumberg believes that a famous psychology experiment by E.L. Thorndike helps illustrate this instinctive reaction to search desperately for an escape. Thorndike, based at a division of Columbia University for most of his career, conducted an experiment in the 1890s with cats and various "puzzle-boxes" with doors held shut by a simple latch or other mechanism. In the experiments, a cat was placed inside a puzzle box, outside of which food had been set within sight. The cat, after failing to reach the food through the wooden cage bars, would walk around the box and eventually bump the latch or another device that would open the door. The cat then ate the food, and was placed back in the box. The process began again, and the cat again would eventually bump the latch. This was repeated over and over. Eventually, the cats stopped trying to reach the food through the bars and spent time near the latch. Finally, the cat could open the latch quickly and efficiently. Thorndike, one of the first to conduct laboratory experiments related to animal intelligence, theorized that the cat learned to escape the cage through trial and error. It performed various movements in a random way until some action freed it. But, almost invariably, the cats first acted erratically when placed in the confined space. Thorndike, who died in 1949, wrote:

"[It] tries to squeeze through any opening; it claws and bites at the bars or wire; it thrusts its paws out through any opening and claws at everything it reaches; it continues its efforts when it strikes anything loose and shaky; it may claw at things within the box. It does not pay very much attention to the food outside, but seems simply to strive instinctively to escape from confinement. The vigor with which it struggles is extraordinary. For eight or ten minutes it will claw and bite and squeeze incessantly."

Inside the grain hopper, the men and women would have displayed basic animal instincts for survival. They would have picked at any small opening, hoping against all odds for some chance of escape or, at the very least, for the slightest hint of cooler air. They would have slipped on the angled bottom of the grain car as they tried to stand, groping for an opening. They would have pounded their fists on the railcar, desperate to attract anyone's attention.

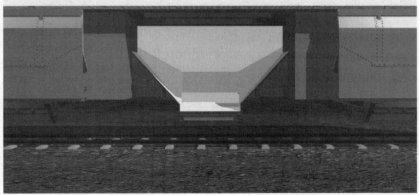

Graphic of grain hopper's configuration.

But the difference between the cat puzzle box experiment and the situation facing the men and women inside the railcar is that "nothing they did had a pleasurable outcome," Blumberg said. "It wasn't a puzzle box. There was no solution."

They would have screamed, but no one would have come.

Investigators would later notice that a piece of the upper hatch door's rubber seal—designed to keep out rain and snow—had been torn away. It is possible that the rubber seal had been damaged before the group ever entered the car. It is just as likely, though, that the members of the trapped group pulled at the rubber, the weakest material in their metal prison. Without special tools, the metal would have been impossible to pierce. It was three-eighths of an inch thick, strong enough to hold a little over 200,000 pounds of grain in its three compartments. In 1987, one man survived an oddly similar situation by using a railroad spike to cut an air hole in a freight car, according to *The New York Times*. The man and eighteen other undocumented immigrants had been trapped inside the railcar until being found by Border Patrol agents in Sierra Blanca, Texas. The other eighteen also died.

Torn rubber seal.

Those inside the grain hopper in 2002 had no such tools. The door's rubber seal may have briefly given them hope, however. Two or more may have worked together to try removing the rubber seal in hopes of opening the overhead door, or at least letting in more air. One person would have had trouble attacking it alone because of the way the car was configured. The slope inside the 13-½ foot-tall compartment started about halfway down. It would have been extremely difficult to stand on the slope and still reach the top hatch door. A ladder was attached to one side of the interior, but stopped just above where the slope began. As a result, the ladder would still be 6-½ to 7 feet above the bottom of the slope, which was at a 45 degree angle. A single person would have had to climb up the slope and reach the ladder. It's likely that someone helped boost another up the slope to the ladder. That person would have climbed up and picked desperately at the rubber seal while clinging to the ladder.

If, or when, a small piece of rubber came loose, perhaps he or she worked more frantically, hoping to at least let in some cooler, less humid air. If there was a bit more fresh air, though, it wouldn't have been enough. And, even with the seal partially removed, the space would have been too narrow to reach far enough through to unlock the hatch door. At some point, whether out of sheer exhaustion, a sense of futility, or the worsening physical coordination that comes with hyperthermia, the person working on the hatch door would have climbed or dropped back down, collapsing in a heap among the others.

The metal bottom they collapsed back to would have been extremely hot, adding to their discomfort and pain. "It would be like sitting on a metal bleacher at a baseball game when it has been in the sun," Kregel explained. Also, the last thing they would have wanted was to be lying against another hot human body, but the space was too small to sit very far apart. The compartment was about 10 feet across at its widest point and the lower half sloped to a narrow bottom square that would have three feet across or slightly smaller. It would have been another bit of agony, touching other hot bodies.

Later, when medical examiners and investigators went through the items found in the railcar, they noted the lack of water containers. They found so many little things—watches, a toothbrush, a purse filled with makeup, coins, identification cards and more—but no water containers. Presumably, the men and women didn't bring any water along. They hadn't expected to be inside for long—maybe a couple hours at the most. And one man in the other railcar had been told there was no need for water during such a short ride. If, however, there *had* been a container of water inside after their brain temperatures began to climb, the railcar occupants likely would have fought over it. They would have reverted to their most basic instincts for survival, battling one another for even a few small sips of water.

Instead, their physical condition continued to worsen. As their core body temperatures climbed, their bodies—along with their brains—would have begun to malfunction. Temperature is a major factor in how well neurons in the brain are able to function, in how efficient they are in sending a signal from one part of the brain to another. The same is true when the brain sends a signal to another part of the body, such as an arm or leg. With their body temperatures climbing dangerously, their neurons would no longer fire perfectly. Their movements would have become less coordinated. They would have stumbled when they tried to stand. Some may have had seizures.

Those men and women who endured the conditions longer—whether because of starting with more fluids or because of having better-conditioned hearts—would have had to watch helplessly as others went into seizures, or began moving and acting erratically.

They would have known this was what was in store for them. Did the two Ferrufino sisters and their niece try to help one another as this happened? Or did their conditions worsen at roughly the same pace, leaving them to battle the unbearable conditions on their own? Did Byron, as one of the youngest, survive longer and have to watch the others near death?

"They would have been falling and failing at different rates, and the people who were not failing as quickly would have just been witnesses to that and known that they were next," Blumberg said. "So those people probably had it worst."

Either way, all would have been spent eventually. If they weren't already lying down on the hot metal bottom of the compartment, it would only be a matter of time before they would have collapsed. They would have begun, one by one, to lose consciousness as all their major bodily systems began to fail. "High temperature can impact every cell in the body. It's not just this gross insult to the brain," Kregel said. "Every cell in the body is getting cooked and proteins are starting to de-nature ... then tissues don't function and organs don't function and then systems don't function. Soon, the whole body doesn't."

Eventually, all would have been unconscious.

A Texas forensic pathologist involved in a related civil court case estimated that the railcar occupants would have lived for 24 to 36 hours. Some investigators have cited a slightly shorter estimated time frame of just under, or around, 24 hours.

The men and women would have slumped against one another in the narrow bottom as the train rattled on toward El Reno, Oklahoma, arriving June 18. The railcar would sit in a rail yard there for nearly four months until being connected to a locomotive on October 11 for a trip to an Iowa grain elevator. But, now, late on June 16—the same day as the early-morning Border Patrol inspection—or sometime before noon on June 17, their hearts would have begun to beat slowly, sluggishly.

In the end, there would have been only the continuing rumble of the train moving along the tracks.

Chapter Nine

The day Byron Acevedo disappeared is etched into his oldest brother's memory.

Eliseo Acevedo remembers how he hadn't showered yet when he called the coyote's number, which his wife had written down after talking to Byron. Dust and sweat from a day of landscaping in New York's summer heat still clung to him. The main thing on Eliseo's mind would normally have been getting a shower after a long day at work. Instead, he was talking to an unfamiliar person about his little brother's unannounced and illegal attempt to reach the United States.

Eliseo pictured the brother who hadn't even been born yet when he left Guatemala. The relationship between the two brothers was good, but it wasn't as close as it could have been. They were together during Eliseo's return visits to Guatemala, but those visits weren't frequent enough to allow them to grow particularly close. In some ways, Eliseo's son, Jesse, who was ten years younger than Byron, may have been closer to Byron. Since Byron was the youngest of the Acevedo aunts and uncles, Jesse tended to gravitate toward him when they visited Guatemala.

"He [Byron] wasn't the ordinary adult. He was the fun guy," Jesse said. "We were never bored with him."

The two boys would spend most of their days outdoors. They would ride horses or go fishing. Byron tried to teach Jesse to swim, the first person Jesse remembers doing so. They played soccer and talked about sports in general. "He was my best friend over there. He was always the most kind person," Jesse said. "I looked up to him because he was the excitement when I went there."

Byron was still a boy himself when Jesse last saw him during a visit to Guatemala. Jesse was 7, and Byron was 17. Byron had asked Jesse what kids in the United States did in their free time. They talked about the various sports that children played in both countries. Byron wanted to know what snow was like. He wanted to know everything about life in the United States.

U.S. citizens often wonder: why don't those coming from Mexico or Central America simply apply for the proper documents instead of entering the United States illegally? First, many do wait—1.1 million immigrants were granted permanent resident status in 2009. For those that choose not to wait, however, the reasons may vary as much as personal circumstances vary. The wait during the application process can be lengthy, ranging from several months to several years, sometimes exceeding five years for certain categories of immigrants.

As with Byron Acevedo and most of the others who ended up inside the railcar, many Central Americans and Mexicans know others who have gone illegally to the United States and had been able to send back enough money to improve things at home. As a result, it is tempting for those concerned about their own financial situation to follow the example of others they know. Instead of spending time and money waiting for an answer to an application, they sometimes decide to hire the smuggler who successfully got their friend into the United States.

It's also important to remember how many millions don't try to come to the United States. Home is still home in the midst of economic troubles, and most have some sentimental ties that are not easily broken. Coming to the United States illegally often means leaving behind children, siblings and parents. Eliseo and Byron Acevedo's parents could apply for documents—and have a good chance of getting them—because their son Eliseo is now a citizen, but have so far declined to do so, and have instead only wanted to visit briefly using tourist visas. They prefer to remain in their native land of Guatemala. A third Ferrufino sister, Reyna, says she would never want to try coming to the United States because she believes Central Americans are looked down upon by U.S. citizens. "We are the slaves" there, she said.

Byron, after asking his young nephew so many questions, would eventually decide to find out about the United States first-hand. The conversation Eliseo had with Byron the night he arrived in the United States left Eliseo worried and frustrated. His little brother was on his way to New York and had explained how he had run short of money, and was at the mercy of the smugglers. He needed another $300 if the men were going to smuggle him to Houston, past the Texas checkpoints that made up a sort of interior border. Eliseo understood that the actual border wasn't always the only difficult crossing. Border Patrol had many checkpoints set up farther in from the border, along major highways. If a person made it past these checkpoints, things got easier.

Byron briefly explained on the phone that night that once he reached Houston, he would call Eliseo back for help with a plane ticket, or to find another way to New York. Eliseo, despite his disappointment in Byron's decision, readily agreed to help. Family was important to him, and he could never stand by when a sibling was in trouble. Byron put one of the smugglers on the phone so Eliseo could find out where to wire the money.

Eliseo jumped in his car and made the drive from his home, then in Mt. Kisco, New York, to the nearest Western Union as soon as it opened the next morning. As he drove, he thought about what his brother might face as he tried to get farther into the United States. He knew that many immigrants trying to enter the country illegally died by putting themselves in dangerous situations. Houston, Eliseo thought, was a good destination. Eliseo considered it a safer city than some for undocumented immigrants. How exactly would Byron get there, though?

By the time Eliseo sent the money and called back on June 14, he was anxious to talk with Byron again. When he called, the smugglers accommodated him. Eliseo pointed out to Byron that, technically, Byron was already inside the United States.

Don't do anything that will put your life in danger, Eliseo urged him. *Don't get into a car trunk, don't get into the back of a semi.*

It didn't cross Eliseo's mind to mention a train. He would later wish it had. He would also wish Byron had been more cautious, had refused to get into a locked railcar. Still, he understands that Byron may have had little choice in how he traveled at that point. If he had refused to take the offered transportation, the smugglers might have simply put him on the streets for the INS to find.

If they catch you, they catch you, Eliseo said. *I'll try to bail you out.*

Byron took his older brother's concerns in stride, asking Eliseo to stop worrying. At least the kid is tough, Eliseo thought. Stubborn too or he would have stayed put as his siblings and parents had asked.

～

That combination of being stubborn and tough helped place Byron in a stash house in southern Texas, where he waited for a group of coyotes to slip him farther into the country. Byron explained to his brother that the attempt to get past the checkpoints was supposed to happen soon, perhaps the next day. Byron again promised to call Eliseo as soon as he reached Houston.

Eliseo called his parents' home in Guatemala, and had the conversation that started his parents' worrying, especially his mother's. The house hadn't had a telephone when Eliseo had left 25 years earlier. When Eliseo found himself stranded in California after entering the United States illegally, so many years before, he'd had to wait weeks for a letter to reach his parents explaining his problem. They then had to walk to a town that had a telephone so they could call him. Eliseo had long since seen to it that his parents had a telephone in their home.

That next day, June 15, Eliseo went to work as usual. He knew Byron might not reach Houston as quickly as he'd hoped. Still, Eliseo was anxious all day. Repeatedly, he called his wife at home to ask if she'd heard anything from Byron. Again and again, it was the same thing: no news. Finally, late that day, he called the number he had for one of the coyotes. Byron hadn't made it through yet, the coyote told Eliseo. He went back to waiting to hear from Byron the next day. Eventually, the phone's silence became unnerving. Eliseo couldn't relax, couldn't sit still. He could only continue to call the single phone number he had and wait for news.

By the time three or four days had passed, Eliseo became convinced that Byron had been arrested, probably by the U.S. Border Patrol. After one week, Eliseo called the smugglers' phone number yet again and demanded information. If some wasn't forthcoming, Eliseo said, he would do something about it. The man promised to check with the person who had loaded them onto the train, but, instead, the phone call was disconnected. From that point on, no one answered the phone when Eliseo tried to call.

Soon after, Eliseo bought a plane ticket to Houston. It was a little over a week since he'd last heard from Byron, and Eliseo was determined to find him. His wife, Norma, had watched how he couldn't relax, how he was stressed and anxious day and night. When Eliseo said he had to keep looking for Byron, she didn't hesitate to add her agreement, even though it meant being on her own with their two young boys for days.

If you need to go, then go.

Do whatever we can do, she told him. Both were thankful that Eliseo was now in the country legally, and could travel freely. Full of worry, Eliseo took the flight to Houston, where he boarded a Greyhound bus and headed for the U.S.-Mexico border. Armed with his little brother's photo, he worked his way north from town to town, checking with immigration detention centers, jails, and other law enforcement offices. Through all of it, Eliseo remained convinced that Byron was simply someplace where he couldn't get to a phone. Jail seemed a likely spot to find him.

Eliseo had promised his parents he would track down Byron, and he wasn't about to give up. That first trip to Texas was a failure, however. No one recognized Byron's photo, and his name wasn't showing up on law enforcement computer databases.

Years later, in 2010, the U.S. Immigration and Customs Enforcement would launch a database designed to make it easier for relatives and friends to locate people held in immigration detention facilities. The program, called the Online Detainee Locator System, is intended to prevent people like Eliseo Acevedo from having to travel or call from one immigration detention facility to another in search of a relative.

In the end, Eliseo returned home disappointed, his search having turned up nothing.

He didn't give up, though. Eliseo took three more trips to Texas that long summer. He added morgues and hospitals to the places he searched, but those trips were also fruitless. By the time he gave up, Eliseo felt as though he had covered nearly the entire state of Texas. He no longer felt so certain that his brother was sitting somewhere in a Texas jail, waiting for help. A far worse possibility was on his mind.

He now knew he might not be able to keep that promise to his parents to bring their youngest child home.

~

Eliseo Acevedo's landscaping truck swerved right as he steered toward the shoulder. He had been on his way to a landscaping job in Chappaqua, New York, but something on the news caught his attention. Once stopped, Eliseo turned up the radio and leaned in to hear the rest of the news report on that October morning in 2002, months after his last trip to Texas.

Numerous bodies found inside a railway car in Iowa, the announcer said as Eliseo's heart pounded. *None have been identified yet.*

His little brother had to be one of the bodies, Eliseo thought. Byron Acevedo had been missing for four months since unexpectedly leaving their parents' Guatemalan farm for Eliseo's place in New York. This was the explanation, Eliseo feared. It had to be. A chill ran through him.

Still, he'd had these fears before when he'd heard in recent months about other disasters befalling a group of undocumented immigrants. Maybe this was just another dead end? Somehow, though, Eliseo couldn't quite convince himself of this. Remembering the load of gravel he had to deliver, Eliseo made the five-minute drive, dumped the rock and returned to the office. He immediately called a pastor friend and shared his suspicions, asking the pastor to make some calls to authorities.

By midday, Eliseo was on the phone with Iowa officials and federal investigators, the very types he would have desperately avoided in the days before he had the proper documents to be in the United States. David Jobes, a special agent with the Iowa Division of Criminal Investigation, remembers talking on the phone with Eliseo Acevedo shortly after the bodies were found. Eliseo was clearly distraught over the possibility that his brother might be among the victims. "He was very apprehensive. He thought it was likely his brother. That was a very frightening thought to him; that his brother died just trying to get into the United States," Jobes said.

During these early calls—as Eliseo shared phone numbers and other information about the smugglers who had taken his little brother across the U.S.-Mexico border—he had his first conversations with an Omaha-based INS investigations supervisor named Alonzo

Martinez. Those early phone calls with Alonzo—when Eliseo frantically described his brother and the journey the younger man had taken—marked the point when the two men began to connect; a friendship began to take root. They would get to know each other better in the coming weeks and months.

That day, however, friendship was the last thing on the mind of either one. The law enforcement officials working on the case wanted to get the investigation moving quickly. For them, Eliseo Acevedo's phone call would become one of the important breaks in a criminal case they were trying to build. These eleven people, though trespassing to enter the country illegally, hadn't locked themselves inside the railcar. Someone would be held responsible.

Chapter Ten

The calls from relatives started within a day and half of the train's departure.

Sometime on June 17, during those first days of waiting, Eliseo Acevedo called the phone number he had for the smuggler he knew only as Alvaro Galicia Castro. He didn't yet know that the name was a fake one used by Licea when receiving payments from undocumented immigrants' relatives via Western Union. The man who answered the phone—presumably Licea—told Eliseo that his brother Byron had been arrested by the Border Patrol near Sarita, Texas. He gave Eliseo a list of others who he said had been arrested at the same time. Eliseo wrote down each name on a piece of paper as Licea listed them, knowing that if he found one of these others in an immigration detention center, he might be close to locating his little brother. Most of those named by Licea would ultimately be accounted for among the dead. That small piece of paper would serve as a key piece of evidence connecting Licea, then calling himself Alvaro Galicia Castro, to some of the victims.

That same day, June 17, a man named Jose Ardon called the same Harlingen, Texas, phone number. No one answered. Jose Ardon was worried about his brother, Domingo Ardon, who had gotten as far as southern Texas after leaving El Salvador. Jose had not heard from Domingo since June 13, when he had called the smugglers' phone to make sure that they had gotten the $300 payment he had sent the previous day. Jose talked to his brother that day. Domingo had told Jose that they had recently tried—unsuccessfully—to board a train, but were planning to try again soon.

Domingo Ardon and Isidro Avila Bueso.

Around this same time, a New York resident named Erasmo Ortega was growing increasingly concerned about the silence that had followed his payment of a smuggling fee for an uncle. Ortega asked his sister to call the smugglers' phone number to ask about their uncle, Isidro Avila Bueso, who had left Honduras in late May 2002. Ortega wrote in a statement about the phone call:

> "My sister spoke with an unidentified individual and asked for my uncle, but this person had no knowledge of my uncle and asked that we contact him if my uncle called. It appeared this person was worried about my uncle. Three or four days later, I called again, and this person told me the same thing. About a week

later, this person called me and gave me two numbers to Immigration to ask for my uncle. I called these numbers, and I was told he was not there. My sister Marlenis called an attorney ... to find my uncle, but she could not find him."

A message finally started telling those who called the smugglers' number that it had been disconnected and was no longer in service. It was then that Eliseo Acevedo's restlessness turned to fear. "After that, I got scared and told my wife, 'I've got to do something.'"

Interviews and evidence collected by investigators suggest that Licea and others involved, such as smuggler Rogelio Hernandez, had their own fears about the true fate of those inside the railcar. They appear to have had their own suspicions as soon as—even before—they got the calls from anxious relatives. Too many clues were starting to suggest that something had gone wrong for the occupants of one of the railcars.

The first clue was that no one from the railcar of eleven had called Licea. The smugglers had their own type of customer-satisfaction guarantee. They offered undocumented immigrants who were caught by Border Patrol another chance—or two or three—to reach Houston without having to pay the smuggling fee again. As a result, those who were caught would almost always be back in touch with Licea, or others in the smuggling operation, within a short period of time. They would either demand their money back or start planning another attempt to reach Houston. The smugglers had heard from many of the 26 who had been in the first railcar, but none of the eleven from the second railcar had called or returned to the stash house. This didn't fit the typical scenario of a Border Patrol apprehension, particularly for those who had hired and been coached by these particular smugglers on how to get through.

Often, Mexicans arrested for being in the United States illegally—assuming they aren't repeat offenders or criminals wanted on other charges—are released within hours of being caught. Border Patrol agents will escort them back to the border and watch them return to their home country. The Mexicans who are escorted back home might try to cross back into the United States within a few hours or days, risking jail time if they are repeatedly caught. The agents can't, however, escort someone from places such as Nicaragua or El Salvador across the border into Mexico because the Mexican government won't typically allow it. Those from Central American countries or any other country besides Mexico—people called "Other Than Mexicans" or OTMs by the agents—are not, after all, their citizens either. To the Mexican government, these OTMs are considered undocumented immigrants in their country just as they are in the United States.

Instead, when U.S. Border Patrol agents catch OTMs, they typically start deportation proceedings, which can be a lengthy process, or hold the person after granting voluntary departure until arrangements have been made for how they will return home. In other words, Central Americans would typically be in custody much longer than Mexicans who had entered the United States illegally.

Knowing this, the smugglers would have coached the eight Central Americans in the railcar to claim they were citizens of Mexico if they were caught by Border Patrol. Licea and his associates had a partial, if not complete, list of those who were inside the railcar. They would have known that many of them were from Central America, but they would have expected the Central Americans in the second grain hopper, such as Byron Acevedo, to return to them shortly by making the claim to be Mexican. Certainly, the three who were actually from Mexico would have shown up at least. But in this case, none showed up.

The second clue that something had gone wrong would likely have come from Licea's associate, who drove along Highway 77 near the tracks, watching what was happening with the train inspection. That man wouldn't have been able to say with 100 percent certainty that both railcars had been emptied. Both Licea and this assistant might have quickly realized that a bad assumption had been made that all those trespassing on the train had been caught.

Court records show that Licea called Arnulfo Flores, the conductor who was providing them train schedules, less than four hours after the train left Harlingen on the night of June 15. In fact, records show that Flores received six phone calls from Licea's phone between 1 a.m. and 2 a.m. on June 16. The Border Patrol had stopped the train around 1 a.m.

Flores, conductor on another train that night, remembers at least three phone calls around that time from Licea, and perhaps one from an associate of Licea's. Flores admits that it's hard to remember exactly how many phone calls he got, or when the calls came. He believes, though, that the first call came when he either wasn't alone or was too busy with work to talk. He told Licea they would have to talk later. Licea and Flores did talk again, and at greater length, around 6 a.m., five hours after the Border Patrol inspection. Licea was "a little antsy" at that time, Flores said. "He was like, 'Hey, I need to find a train. I lost a train.'" Flores looked up the train's location on the Union Pacific computers. The train had reached Kingsville, Flores told Licea.

Trains pass defect detectors as they travel along tracks. These detectors scan the passing trains for possible overheating around the axle bearings. Some of these detectors can also record information such as train number, track number, and train speed. This information can be sent automatically by radio signal to the train crews. As a result,

Flores could easily find out by logging into a Union Pacific computer when a train had reached the location of a certain detector, thereby tracking its progress. The information was easily accessible for Union Pacific employees, Flores said. Many railroad workers had this type of access. The smugglers who called that night knew Flores could get this information, and knew it would give them a better chance of finding the train they had lost.

Flores believes that he and Licea talked again that day, June 16, perhaps sometime in the afternoon. By 3 p.m., the train had already left Kingsville, heading to Odem, Texas. Flores remembers Licea acting more nervous about the fate of the missing people. Still, Flores insists that Licea would not have known for certain that the eleven hadn't simply been arrested and held by Border Patrol. Licea might have had suspicions, but no way to know for sure that the eleven immigrants were facing a far worse fate. "I think they wanted to find out that day if the people were on there," Flores said. "I think maybe past 24 or 48 hours, I think after that it didn't really matter. They just kind of blew it off."

Licea, who was in federal prison in Texas at the time this book was published, declined to be interviewed. In court appearances, he doesn't deny being involved in smuggling some of the people and keeping them in a stash house. But he has argued that he should not be held responsible for the deaths because he was not one of those present to actually load them and close the hatch door that night.

Licea had the following conversation with U.S. District Court Judge Kenneth Hoyt during a March 2004 appearance in Houston:

Hoyt: "You are charged with conspiracy to harbor and transport undocumented aliens that resulted in the deaths of an individual. What is that about? What happened?"

Licea: "What do you mean?"

Hoyt: "Well, that is what I'm asking you. What happened? Why are you charged with this offense?"

Licea: "Because I helped in the transportation of those people. I picked them up from the river. I put them in a house in Harlingen and I transported them all the way to Raymondville, and I delivered them to a person there. And it was the other people that got them on the train."

Hoyt: "All right. So you were not at the part of this journey where they were put on the train and eventually died?"

Licea: "I was not present."

Hoyt: "That is what I understood you to say.... . This is what the government would need to prove as I understand it: that you and at least one other person made an agreement to commit the crimes of harboring and transporting undocumented aliens for the purpose of financial gain, commercial advantage. Number two, that you knew the unlawful purpose of the agreement and yet you joined in it willfully, that is, no one forced you to, with the intent to accomplish it. That is, to further that purpose. Number three, that one of the conspirators, either yourself or someone else, during the existence of the conspiracy, knowingly committed an act—an act similar or like the one described in the indictment—in order to accomplish the objective of the conspiracy, and that as a consequence of the existence of the conspiracy and the acts carried out in furtherance of the conspiracy, the death of a person resulted."

The judge then described the evidence connecting Licea to the smuggling of at least six of the eleven, and outlined how at least three others were kept in stash houses under Licea's control. Licea would ultimately enter a guilty plea, which he has since fought to withdraw.

~

Most of the investigators interviewed believe that Licea was concerned enough in those early hours that he or his associates made at least a minimal effort to find the train to make sure the grain hopper had been emptied. But there would have been problems with their search. First, the smugglers' assistants and sometimes the smugglers themselves— Licea included—were undocumented immigrants. As a result, many in the smuggling operation could not go beyond the automobile checkpoint near Sarita to try to find the train. By 5:20 a.m., the train had already gone beyond the checkpoint and was in or near Kingsville, which is about 100 miles north of Harlingen. Other assistants, and smugglers' girlfriends or wives were legal U.S. residents or citizens, however, and could travel past the checkpoint to Kingsville.

If someone did make the trip and managed to catch up with the train, they would have run into trouble finding the specific grain hopper that held the eleven. Smugglers often mark a railcar with spray paint so they can later find it. Alternatively, they might enter the railcar's identification number into a cell phone so they have it later if they should need it. The smugglers in this case either didn't record that serial number, or lost it, explained Gabe Bustamante, who was then part of a Border Patrol anti-smuggling unit involved in the case.

The train also took a different route than the smugglers expected. They thought it would head toward Victoria and ultimately on a northeasterly route to Houston, but this particular train headed more directly north, eventually going through Fort Worth. The train left Kingsville and traveled the 35 miles to Odem, Texas. It left Odem just after 5 p.m. on June 16, according to the Union Pacific track records.

The smugglers thought something was wrong, especially once relatives started calling the next day (and perhaps earlier), but weren't sure exactly how wrong. Yet, none of the smugglers called authorities to report their suspicions in those first hours after the Border Patrol inspection, not even anonymously. Licea and the others didn't call that day or early the following day, when there might have been a chance of saving some, or all, of the eleven. Flores, the conductor, never called authorities either, even though he knew about the possibility of someone being inside a railcar by at least 6 a.m. that day.

Presumably, they all worried about implicating themselves.

～

Union Pacific, Flores' employer at the time, was sued in 2004 by attorneys representing ten of the victims' families (relatives of Mercedes Guido Lorente from Nicaragua, the eleventh victim, were not included because of the belief that she was working with one of the smugglers). Two attorneys from McAllen, Texas, had approached most of the families. The families went along. Some felt a bit reluctant about seeking money in this manner, but ultimately agreed.

Kevin Young, whose San Antonio law firm later joined the McAllen attorneys on the case, acknowledged that the undocumented immigrants were trespassers on the train. The case was different, however, because Flores, then a Union Pacific conductor, was connected with the smuggling operation. The lawsuit against Union Pacific, whose railroad franchise covers twenty-three states, focused on the fact that Flores—as a Union Pacific employee—had a duty to report when someone's life might be endangered. The company even had an anonymous safety tip line. Flores knew people were possibly trespassing on a Union Pacific train when he got the phone calls from the smuggler Licea. He didn't pass on that information to his employer, Union Pacific, as the lawsuit alleges he was obligated to do.

"The easiest way for him to have done that, and to have avoided any complications for himself because he was a participant in this scheme to smuggle people for money, would have been to call a 1-800 number that the Union Pacific has for situations like this and similar situations," said Grant McFarland, another attorney representing the families. "And he didn't do that. He chose instead to keep quiet and put his own personal interests ahead of the lives of eleven people."

A company can be held responsible for its employees, which is the reason the families' attorneys felt Union Pacific had some liability. Union Pacific paid $1.5 million to settle the case without admitting liability, court records show. Roughly half went to attorneys and litigation costs. The survivors of the ten divided the remaining $750,000. The amounts given to each parent, spouse or child ranged from $4,200 to $65,000. Anthony Matulewicz, one of the McAllen attorneys, said that the money given to surviving relatives might not seem like a lot in the United States, but it would be significant to many Central Americans considering the extreme poverty most face.

Union Pacific attorneys and officials declined to be interviewed about this case.

Mark K. Reed, a former INS supervisor who now consults on border enforcement issues, did background research for Union Pacific on the case after leaving the INS. He said the civil suit didn't surprise him. "Everybody wants to be a victim, and everybody wants a scapegoat and, in this case, it's Union Pacific that was placed in that position when it should have been the smugglers," Reed said.

Alonzo Martinez had mixed feelings on the civil case. "There are thousands of miles (of track) throughout the United States. I know that there are responsibilities for the railroad, like there are for me with my backyard, but can I keep everybody out? I can't," Alonzo said. "But am I supposed to do something to at least try to minimize it? Of course, the answer is yes. And I'm speaking about myself. But the conductor himself, he was negligent, he was criminal in his behavior. He knew that he was selling information to an illegal organization."

Flores said that he didn't call because he never had definitive proof that anyone's life was in danger. He argues that it was possible that the missing men and women might have been arrested and held by Border Patrol.

Eventually, perhaps after a week or two passed, the smugglers seemed to put it out of their minds, Alonzo said. "They went on with business." Some of them, including Licea, did change the false names they were using to collect Western Union payments, or changed or dropped phone numbers. But most went on with the work of smuggling undocumented immigrants into the U.S. interior.

For a while, things seemed to settle back into a routine for the coyotes. Then, four months later, the news of bodies being found inside a railcar in Iowa hit the airwaves.

The smugglers got scared.

These bodies inside a railcar, they suspected, were the people lost so many weeks ago.

Chapter Eleven

B.J. Schany, the Iowan who discovered the bodies, didn't notice a foul odor when he opened the grain hopper door that October afternoon. Several media outlets that covered the discovery suggested that it was, in part, the smell of death which drew Schany's attention to the railcar. Or that he was hit with it as soon as he opened the door. But that wasn't the case. Schany doesn't remember an odor other than perhaps the usual smell of spoiling field corn. Any stench present earlier in the process of decomposition may have been muted after the bodies had essentially baked for months, undisturbed in the summer and early fall heat of an Oklahoma rail yard, where the grain hopper had been parked.

Rick Zimmerman, an assistant chief with the Des Moines Fire Department, also remembers noting the lack of a significant odor as he and other firefighters used a special torch to cut open the railcar's side, a step deemed necessary to provide easier access to the crime scene. He knew there were numerous bodies inside, and had expected to smell something.

Firefighter torching open the hopper's side.

Once the forensic team entered the railcar and began removing bodies and evidence, however, the odor was released with a vengeance. Even some of those in law enforcement, who at least occasionally encountered decomposed bodies, noted how brutal the odor was once the railcar's contents were disturbed. Many of those who climbed inside the grain hopper or worked next to it in the following hours and days reeled from the smell, some needing frequent breaks to escape to fresher air.

Estela Biesemeyer, with the Des Moines INS office, never got inside the railcar when it was parked in Des Moines, but instead helped sort through evidence in tents outside the state medical examiner's building. Yet, she remembers how the smell clung to her, how it seemed to stick with her long after she left the evidence area. "It was horrible," Biesemeyer remembers. "For days, I thought I had that smell on me. I kept saying to my husband, 'Do I smell?' But he'd say, 'No.'"

Human bodies go through five stages of decomposition. The length of time it takes for those stages to occur can vary from a few days to years, depending on the surrounding conditions. The first stage—the "fresh" stage—primarily involves chemical changes at the cellular level. Cells and organs begin to break down. The body's temperature changes to match the temperature of the surrounding environment. During the second stage, putrefaction, the decomposing body begins to change in color and odor. Bloating also happens, forcing liquids out of the body. The person becomes difficult to recognize because of the facial swelling.

The third stage, black putrefaction, involves the body color darkening from the greenish color it took on during the second stage. The body cavity also breaks open, releasing gases that were building up in the abdomen. The odor intensifies. Insects, which would have been present before, are particularly active now. Bones begin to show. The fourth stage is butyric fermentation, or the start of mummification. This is when the body begins to dry out, and the odor begins to lessen. The fifth and final stage is dry decay, or skeletonization. This longest-lasting phase happens when the last of the soft tissue is gone from the body. It involves the deterioration of the bones.

The bodies found in the railcar were in the fourth or fifth stages of decomposition: mummification and skeletonization, according to Dr. Dennis F. Klein, Iowa's deputy state medical examiner.

Craig Friedrichs, then with the Crawford County Sheriff's Office, watched as state and federal officials worked the crime scene. Friedrichs, who had ridden along as the railcar was taken to Des Moines during the night, was waiting for another deputy to pick him up for a ride home. Instead of sleeping that morning at a Des Moines hotel, he watched the state and federal investigators work.

"It was a trying effort for them. It was just downright nasty in there," Friedrichs said. The forensic team took short shifts inside the railcar, getting out briefly before returning. "I even kind of backed off and yet they stayed right in there close," Friedrichs said.

He described the compartment bottom as being covered with a thick clay-like substance that also covered much of the evidence they pulled out. Eventually, the bodies—better described as skeletons— were removed and taken with the other evidence collected to the Iowa Office of State Medical Examiner, which conducts more than 700 autopsies most years. It is extremely rare for the office to handle so many related deaths at a time, however, Klein said. He doesn't remember another such case during his decade with the office that involved so many connected homicides.

Within days of the bodies being discovered, the medical examiner had some general information about the victims, such as gender (at first, they thought there were five women instead of four), height, and estimated ages. The medical examiners in Iowa didn't feel they could give a very accurate time of death because of the condition of the bodies. Any such estimate had to stem, in part, from information and evidence collected during the related investigation. Eventually, the medical examiners ruled that the cause of death was hyperthermia and dehydration.

The manner of death was ruled as homicide. In Iowa, all deaths are listed as one of the following manners of death: natural, suicide, accident, homicide or undetermined. For the purposes of a death certificate, homicide simply means that the person died at the hands of another person. The intent of the responsible person isn't usually considered when determining the manner as it might be if a homicide case ended up in the courts.

Putting names to the bodies would be more difficult than coming up with the cause of death. Even in cases where documents or identification cards were found, it was still difficult to connect those documents with a particular body. Between the general information about the bodies from the medical examiner, the evidence collected inside the railcar, and phone calls from people like Eliseo Acevedo, the investigators began to make progress.

Eliseo had kept the list of names of undocumented immigrants who Licea had said might have been arrested with Eliseo's little brother. That list helped. Still, it quickly became apparent that someone would need to travel outside the United States to obtain DNA samples from relatives of those believed to be among the victims.

FBI Special Agent Rosemary Amerena was one of those people who would travel to wrap up the identification of the bodies. Then based in the border town of Brownsville, Texas, Amerena was considered a public corruption specialist. She also worked on cases involving the smuggling of undocumented immigrants. Amerena, who spent most of her childhood in El Paso, joined the so-called "Denison 11" investigative team that fall of 2002, and was the only FBI agent who ended up working on the case more than a few days.

By the time Amerena got involved, the U.S. Attorney's Office in Cedar Rapids, Iowa, had decided that any attempt to prosecute someone in connection with the deaths should be handled in southern Texas. Not only had the train entered the United States there, but the undocumented immigrants had been loaded inside the grain hopper there. It is also likely that the eleven died while the train was still in Texas. Any crime—such as the illegal smuggling of humans—would have happened in that area. It would be prosecuted by the U.S. Attorney's Office in the southern district of Texas, based in Houston.

The FBI, which has a DNA lab, would be responsible for confirming the victims' identities. The Iowa medical examiners extracted DNA, or deoxyribonucleic acid, samples from the femur bones of some victims. In other cases, samples were obtained from a tooth.

Rosemary Amerena.

Having successfully obtained DNA samples from all eleven bodies, the investigators needed DNA from surviving relatives. The list of possible victims included people from five countries: Mexico, Guatemala, Honduras, Nicaragua, and El Salvador. U.S. consulate or embassy representatives in the various countries helped locate the families of the possible victims, and made arrangements for Amerena and others on the team to meet them. The families of the Mexicans agreed to meet investigators in Brownsville. The Mexican victims included the two cousins, Roberto and Omar, as well also Juan Enrique Reyes Meza, a man from Montemorelos in Nuevo León, Mexico. Reyes had left his home in mid-May, eventually reaching Harlingen, where his brother, living in Georgia, wired him money for the smugglers. His relatives would come to nearby Brownsville months later to speak with authorities and provide the needed DNA sample. Reaching the families in the four Central American countries wouldn't be so simple. Amerena remembers being warned by Alonzo to be prepared for the remoteness she might encounter. He told her, only half-jokingly, that she might be riding a donkey up a mountain to reach a home at some point. Amerena had never been to Central America before, and, even as an FBI agent who had seen a lot, was surprised by the degree of poverty she encountered.

Juan Enrique Reyes Meza and Pedro Amador Lopez.

Amerena traveled to Honduras in late November 2002 with another member of the team, a then-INS senior special agent Luis Massad. Honduras was the country from which the most victims— five of the eleven—came. The relatives of two missing men, Pedro Amador Lopez and Isidro Avila Bueso, traveled from their respective communities to meet Amerena and Massad in the capital city of Tegucigalpa, a journey that took some of them more than eight hours by bus. Initially, Amerena and Massad weren't even certain that Isidro Avila Bueso's family would show up. The investigators had called a store near the family's home because it had a phone and the family apparently did not. They had left a message explaining what relatives they would need to be in Tegucigalpa on a certain date. In the end, the family did arrive, and Amerena got the DNA sample she needed.

The three other victims from Honduras were the two sisters, Lely Ferrufino, 36, and Rosibel Ferrufino, 33, and their niece, Lesly "Esmeralda" Ferrufino, 17, the youngest in the railcar. A third sister who lived in Tegucigalpa had called her mother, Obdulia Ferrufino Burgos, and asked her to come from their home area to meet the investigators. Obdulia Ferrufino traveled about five hours to reach the capital. When she arrived, however, Amerena realized there was a problem. The mitochondrial DNA samples needed to come from someone tied to the mother's side of the family, typically either the mother herself or a sibling. This wasn't a problem in trying to identify Rosibel and Lely since it was their mother, Obdulia, who had come to Tegucigalpa. Lesly, however, was Obdulia's granddaughter, the daughter of her son. They didn't have the maternal link they needed.

The Ferrufino relatives then tried unsuccessfully to locate Lesly's

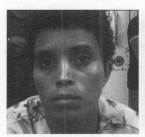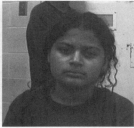

Lely Ferrufino, Lesly Ferrufino, Rosibel Ferrufino.

mother by calling around. Having little luck, the entire group, including Amerena, made the long journey back to the grandmother's home, which was near a small village in a mountainous area outside of Choluteca, Honduras.

The Ferrufino home was a very simple wood and adobe structure. The family cooked using an open fire, and slept in hammocks. They didn't have electricity. They drew water by hand from their well. Amerena remembers how, at one point, the grandmother, Obdulia, took a drink of water as they were talking. Afterward, she took the remaining water and simply dumped it on the floor, which was packed dirt. The grandmother explained that she had a habit of dumping water on the unfinished floor to keep the dust down. This small act stood out to Amerena as a symbol of what a different place she grew up in compared to the Ferrufino women. For Amerena, the experience was an eye opener.

Many U.S. citizens understand what motivates Central Americans and other immigrants to leave their homelands. Some empathize. But, for those living in the United States—even an FBI agent—it may be difficult to truly understand their daily lives until seen first-hand.

House in Honduras.

While poverty statistics aren't perfect when comparing one country to another, they do illustrate how poverty becomes commonplace in many parts of Central America. In 2006, seven out of ten people (71.5 percent) in Honduras were living without access to basic provisions, according to the Economic Commission for Latin America and the Caribbean. Mexico had a poverty rate of 31.7 percent that same year. Poverty in the United States typically falls in the 12 to 17 percent range.

⌣

The United States, in the years after World War II, continued to send mixed messages to immigrants wanting to come to the United States. By 1954, an aggressive program called "Operation Wetback" was begun to again try deporting undocumented immigrants who had come from Mexico. Some politicians were concerned with the large number of immigrants entering the country illegally, and frustrated that other government officials didn't seem to take the problem seriously. One retired Border Patrol veteran, Joseph White, said that in the early 1950s, when many undocumented Mexicans were working for cotton growers, some senior U.S. officials overseeing immigration enforcement "had friends among the ranchers" and agents "did not dare" arrest their illegal workers, according to the *Christian Science Monitor*. By late July of 1954, however, more than 50,000 were reportedly deported from California and Arizona, the states where the "Operation Wetback" effort was started because there appeared to be more support. An estimated 488,000 left voluntarily to avoid arrest. The number continued to climb in the following months, and the INS claimed that 1.3 million were either deported or chose to leave as a result of the program.

Just over a decade later, as the Civil Rights Movement gained momentum, the 1965 Immigration and Nationality Act tried to treat immigrants from various parts of the world more equally. Previously, the law had limited people from certain regions of the world more than those from others.

Mexico, which had been enjoying some rapid industrialization, entered a roughly 20-year period of economic struggles starting in 1976. At the same time, civil wars and natural disasters were plaguing Central America. In El Salvador, the strife was between the military-led government and the Farabundo Marti National Liberation Front

(FMLF) coalition, an umbrella organization of five left-wing militias. The violence in El Salvador carried over to neighboring countries, including Honduras, at various times in the long-running conflict, which ended around 1990. Guatemala had its own civil war. The violence there—largely tied to political events and guerrilla groups—continued in a big way for many years. In Nicaragua, the Sandinista Revolution took place in 1979. For years, the Sandinista National Liberation Front resisted the U.S.-supported Contras.

During those years, both Central America and Mexico had a large number of people leave, with or without permission, to the United States, where they typically had little trouble finding work. By the 1990s, legal immigration rates had nearly doubled. The period between 2000 and 2005 saw 7.9 million new immigrants arrive—about half illegally—making it the highest five-year period of immigration in the nation's history, according to Census Bureau data.

The estimated foreign-born population in the United States—including those who came legally and illegally—topped 38 million in 2008, according to the Pew Hispanic Center. This is the highest number ever recorded in American history. (At roughly 12 percent of the population, however, we have not reached the record percentage of 14.8 percent from 1890) In 1970, for example, first-generation immigrants numbered 9.6 million. The largest number of first-generation immigrants came from Mexico, followed by the region of South and East Asia.

When immigrants come from Mexico or Central America now, they are more likely to remain. They are less likely to act as migrant workers, who travel north to work for brief periods in construction, agriculture or other industries before returning home. More often, one family member moves first—perhaps after several shorter work trips—and then tries to get the rest of the family into the country.

Rosibel Ferrufino, one of the sisters from Honduras who died in the hopper, had been living in Virginia, cleaning apartments to make a living while her five children remained with their grandmother in Honduras. Rosibel had returned to Honduras to escort her niece and her sister, Lely, who left behind three children, back to the United States, where they had planned to work for a while before returning home. The women, two of whom were single mothers, knew they could make enough working for a few months in the United States to feed themselves, their children, and other family members for a much longer period.

As she visited the Ferrufino house in Honduras, FBI Agent Amerena worried that she wouldn't come home with the DNA needed to confirm the identity of the granddaughter, Lesly, who went by "Esmeralda." The girl's mother and father had passed away. The best hope would be to look for a maternal grandmother, but the Ferrufinos believed that this woman lived in a community that would take another two hours of driving to reach. Before they left the Ferrufino house that day, however, a man stopped by. He introduced himself to Amerena; he was Lesly's uncle—a brother to her mother. He provided the necessary maternal link. Amerena had another DNA sample.

During the visit, Obdulia Ferrufino was not only grieving the three women—she was certain they were dead—but also worrying about how she would feed the eight children. Obdulia wasn't particularly worried about prosecuting anyone in connection with the deaths. The information she provided about the smugglers who helped the women reach Mexico and the United States was vague. "She didn't want to deal with it. She was very advanced in years [but was] a very strong woman," Amerena said. "Her biggest concern, after knowing how to get those bodies back, was what to do with the kids."

The surviving Ferrufino relatives still think about what the end would have been like for the three women. "They probably were dying hugging—the three of them—thinking of their kids, and also Esmeralda thinking of her grandma," said Reyna, another sister.

As the head of the household, Obdulia had to find a way to support the children. She sometimes sold a type of empanada pastry filled with fruit jam along a main road to scrape together what money she could. She made cheese to sell, as well.

Children who live in rural areas like the Ferrufino children are 2-1/2 times more at risk of their growth falling behind than those living in urban areas, according to Encuesta Nacional de Demografia y Salud (ENDESA). Children undernourished during their first two years of life are less likely to complete school and will earn, on average, 10 to 17 percent less income when grown compared to those who were well-nourished as children, according to the World Bank.

Children of Lely Ferrufino and Rosibel Ferrufino, 2002.

The percentage of young children (under 5) deemed underweight in Honduras has shown noticeable improvement since 1996, dropping from 19 percent to 9 percent ten years later. In Guatemala, the number improved only slightly and remained a relatively high 18 percent. In Mexico, just 3 percent of young children are considered underweight. One percent of young children in the United States are considered underweight, the World Bank reported.

Central America, the poorest region in the hemisphere, is still plagued by the after-effects of civil wars, political upheavals, and natural disasters it endured over the last three decades. The region has an imbalance in earnings. In Guatemala, for example, the poorest 20 percent of the population received three percent of the national income, while the top 20 percent of the wealthiest people accounted for 58 percent of the national income.

One Texan, who traveled to Guatemala for missionary work, described online the two sharply contrasting worlds she saw when traveling through the country. The images associated with those contrasting worlds stuck in her mind, just as Amerena couldn't forget how a woman in Honduras dumped her drink on her dirt floor. The Texan wrote:

> "The first morning, we arose early to see the sun coming up against the towering volcano Fuego in Antigua, while sipping Café con Leche at a rooftop table. But the glass high-rises and BMW's of the City and the Spanish Colonial villas of Antigua turned to cinder block structures and chicken buses just outside of town. Further out were bicycles and adobe houses, or bare feet and cornstalk huts. My first day there, I was shocked at the level of poverty I saw all around me."

Chapter Twelve

Eliseo Acevedo had almost immediately sensed, upon hearing the radio news reports about bodies in a train, that his brother was among the dead. Once he heard that the train had entered the country around the same time that his brother had disappeared, Eliseo's certainty grew. Although the identification of the bodies hadn't yet been confirmed that fall of 2002, he found it nearly impossible to hope any longer for a better answer. At the same time, he couldn't stand to steal the last bit of hope from his parents, his mother in particular.

As a result, he made plans to go with Amerena, of the FBI, as she traveled to his parents' home near Chiquimula, Guatemala, in mid-November 2002. Eliseo convinced Amerena to avoid discussing too directly the reason for the visit. Eliseo's mother's health had worsened as she worried about the ongoing silence following Byron's departure. He didn't want to add more stress until they were certain that Byron was among the dead. Amerena remembers worrying that it would be awkward to swab the woman's mouth for a DNA sample without explaining, but she agreed to comply with Eliseo's request. She understood.

Amerena was impressed by the beautiful terrain during the four-hour drive from the capital to the Acevedo home. She also noticed the striking degree of poverty in the countryside, which became gradually less populated as they traveled farther from the capital.

Guatemala has had more than its share of violence and unrest. Eliseo remembers the years of civil war that were part of his childhood in the 1960s. A military coup of young army officers tried to overthrow Guatemala's president in 1960 because of his leadership style and ties to the United States. The plan failed, but the junior officers fled to the mountains and sought help from Fidel Castro of Cuba. The group turned into a guerilla movement. The 36-year civil war began, and would eventually cost more than 200,000 lives. "It wasn't as bad in our area as in some parts of Guatemala, but you would still see people dying," Eliseo said. The country's civil war ended in 1996, but Guatemala still struggles with very high crime rates. Violent crimes such as kidnapping, carjacking, and murder are relatively common.

Less than five years after Byron disappeared, a second brother of Eliseo's would disappear. Carlos Acevedo was kidnapped from his home by a group of more than a dozen heavily-armed men. Eliseo went to Guatemala, facing the horror of hunting for a missing brother yet again. He had to identify a body found miles away in a field as that of his brother. Carlos had worked in the United States at an auto body shop after coming to the country illegally. After he returned home, Carlos started his own auto body shop in Guatemala. No one was arrested in connection with the death, but Eliseo suspects it was done by someone who didn't like Carlos' auto repair shop competing with their own business.

In late July 2010, it happened all over again. Alida Acevedo Pérez, one of Eliseo's sisters, was gunned down at her home in Ocós, Guatemala, near the border with Mexico. Eliseo said that Alida ran a hotel in the town, and had been the focus of an earlier assassination attempt by people Eliseo described as her competitors. She had hired bodyguards as a result, but even her two bodyguards couldn't save her. Eliseo said three men checked in as guests in her hotel, which adjoined her home, and carried out the attack the next day. The San Marcos, Guatemala, newspaper *La Noticia* reported that one of the bodyguards answered when someone came to the door of Alida Acevedo's home. That bodyguard was gunned down. The three then shot at a second bodyguard before turning and shooting Alida Acevedo, who was resting in a hammock, the newspaper reported. The attackers fled the area. Eliseo is convinced the attack was orchestrated by the same people who tried to kill her before.

If you have too much money in Guatemala, Eliseo said, you are in trouble. If you have too little money, you are in trouble. "That is how it is in our country," he said.

In Chiquimula, that November of 2002, Amerena and Eliseo Acevedo arrived around noon at the Acevedo home. Eliseo's mother, Maria, insisted they sit down for a meal. She served chicken, and Amerena thought it was the best she'd had in her life, but found it odd when a live chicken walked by as they ate. The house, though humble, was nicer than many. The family no longer struggled to buy the basics, such as food and clothing. It was, Amerena understood, partially because of the money Eliseo had been able to send to the family during his years of working in the United States. The family also owned land, which typically meant a better standard of living. Nearly half of the 200-plus acres had been passed to Eliseo's father, Sixto, from his own father. Sixto had purchased the rest of the land. They farmed the land, and raised livestock.

During the visit, Eliseo explained to his mother that a DNA test might be a way to rule Byron out among the victims, rather than focusing on how it was more likely a confirmation. Amerena remained quiet, not wanting to say something that would add to the older woman's depression. She didn't want to be the one to put the image in Maria's mind of her son suffering inside that railcar.

~

Amerena's December trips to El Salvador and Nicaragua went smoothly. In El Salvador, Amerena met with the emotional parents of Domingo Ardon Sibrian in the capital city of San Salvador. Though distraught, the man's parents took time to tell Amerena a little about their son. In Managua, the capital of Nicaragua, she met briefly with the children of Mercedes Gertrudis Guido Lorente, the woman suspected of having worked as a guide for one of the smugglers. They explained how their mother hadn't kept in touch.

Eventually, and perhaps against the odds, Amerena got all the necessary comparison DNA samples, and all eleven bodies were officially identified. It took more than seven months.

Once the identities of the bodies were confirmed in spring of 2003, they needed to be returned home to families. Most of the families were facing expenses of at least $2,000. The bodies had been in cold storage at the state medical examiner's office since they had been found, and over time, the federal government's own bill was increasing as it had to pay the state for storage.

The Mexican government agreed to cover the cost of returning the remains of its three citizens. Eliseo Acevedo paid to have Byron's body returned to Guatemala. It wasn't so simple with the remaining seven bodies, however. The respective governments of the various home countries were not willing to pick up the expense. And, for most of the families, the money wasn't something they could come up with so quickly, particularly since many of them had drained any savings in paying the smugglers' fees. They might need years to save enough to get their relative's remains returned.

Amerena, who had met the various Central American families, wondered how they would ever manage to get the bodies back. She had seen the level of poverty first-hand, and knew that the estimated cost of sending the bodies home would be nearly insurmountable for most. It would certainly take many months. The Ferrufino family in Honduras, in particular, would struggle with the cost of claiming three bodies. Obdulia Ferrufino was determined do it, though, she told Amerena, even if it meant working to save for years while trying to feed her eight grandchildren. She, like many others, needed closure. For religious reasons, many wanted their relatives to have burials at home, and were opposed to the idea of cremation.

Amerena realized that the families' dilemmas also created a problem for the U.S. government: if the families couldn't come up with the money quickly, the taxpayers would ultimately be stuck with a much-larger bill, a year or more later. Amerena decided to do a cost analysis to share with her supervisors, examining whether it made more sense to keep paying for the storage while waiting for the families to raise the money to have the bodies returned, or simply redirect that money toward sending the bodies back. In the end, she estimated that it would cost the U.S. government about $20,000 to return the remaining bodies. Unless the families all came up with the necessary money relatively quickly, paying to send them home would save the government money.

Ultimately, the plan was approved by Amerena's supervisors, and the U.S. government sent the remaining bodies home. Obdulia Ferrufino, though a proud woman, realized this might be her only chance to get her daughters and granddaughter home. The Ferrufino women's bodies were finally home in late July 2003. Rosibel's and Lely's children still remember their mothers, but the family rarely discusses their deaths. "We don't talk about that because it's very painful," said their sister Reyna.

Around this time, Union Pacific offered to pick up the bill for the cost of returning a single body home. When the money arrived at Dunn's Funeral Home in Des Moines, which was handling the arrangements for returning most of the bodies, the Mexican and U.S. governments had already paid for all the expenses except one: the bill picked up by Eliseo Acevedo to get his little brother home. The funeral home sent the money to Eliseo to partially reimburse him for the expenses he had covered, said Amy Sweet, a mortician at Dunn's.

Byron's was the first body released from Dunn's, in May 2003. He would be home almost one year after he had left.

On July 31, 2003, members of U.S. Attorney's Offices in Iowa and Texas held a press conference in Des Moines to release not only the names of the victims, but to also announce that a federal grand jury in Houston had charged three men for their alleged role in the smuggling operation. Flores, the former conductor, had also been charged in a criminal complaint by that time. Several state and local officials attending the press conference, including then-Crawford

County Sheriff Tom Hogan, said they had doubted the bodies would ever all be identified.

"I'm amazed," Hogan told *The Des Moines Register* after the press conference in the Des Moines rail yard, where the bodies had been removed from the railcar the previous fall. "I didn't think there was a chance."

Chapter Thirteen

Alonzo Martinez was involved in hundreds of cases during his years in immigration enforcement, whether under the auspices of the U.S. Border Patrol, Immigration and Naturalization Service or, eventually, Immigration and Customs Enforcement. He had gone undercover to gather evidence against drug dealers, sometimes assisting other federal agencies needing someone fluent in Spanish. He had investigated human smuggling operations, as well as the most common cases of illegal entry into the country.

Typically, he kept a professional distance. This was, in part, because most cases moved through his life so quickly that he didn't have time to make many, if any, personal connections. The cases were handed off to federal prosecutors, and Alonzo moved on to something else. He only rarely got to know victims of crime, or the victims' relatives. Instead, he had conversations with drug dealers, smugglers, and many undocumented immigrants. The fact that he made few connections was the result of a deliberate effort on his part to maintain a professional distance. "You see so much and you can't take it home with you," he said.

At home, Alonzo talked very little about what he did during his work day. Rather, he wanted to focus on his family when he was home. His wife, Griselda, remembers attending a birthday party for a friend at some point early in her husband's career. The agents in attendance started telling stories of various arrests and close calls on the job. As Griselda listened, she was stunned to hear how truly dangerous her husband's work was. She understood, though, how much Alonzo thrived in his job, particularly when he worked for Border Patrol in the desert. He came alive when he went to work, she felt.

It was only occasionally that a case would become more personal for Alonzo. The "Denison 11" case was one of those. This particular case, arriving late in his career, would stay with Alonzo more than any other had. "This is just something you never forget. You never put it out of your mind," he said. "I've had nothing like this in my career."

The victims, who had started out as anonymous bodies, gradually became real people. This was especially true with Byron Acevedo. Over the many months it took to confirm the identity of the victims and build a criminal case against those tied to the smuggling operation, Alonzo Martinez talked frequently with Byron's oldest brother, Eliseo. The conversations made Byron real for Alonzo. He began to understand the young boy who had grown up watching his older siblings head off into the world, and how the boy yearned for the same. He understood how Byron was a hard worker, a proud young man who wanted to buy nice things with money that he had earned himself. He didn't want to sit by as his older siblings sent him gifts to keep him happy on their parents' farm.

Alonzo also began to understand Eliseo. He saw how Eliseo carried some guilt for not having had the chance to know his youngest brother better. Although Eliseo traveled to Guatemala relatively often once he had his documents, Eliseo still missed a lot of time with Byron. Alonzo believes that Eliseo also felt guilty that he was living the life that his little brother found so tempting—tempting enough to attempt a dangerous and illegal journey across two borders.

"Here was his kid brother coming to see the United States and all its wonders," Alonzo said. "I think [Eliseo] was feeling guilty that if he wasn't here, Byron might never have come."

Eliseo Acevedo remembers how well he was treated by Alonzo Martinez and the many other investigators who talked with him over the months and years following the deaths. Alonzo helped Eliseo get his mother, Maria, the necessary documents to visit Eliseo temporarily in New York. (His parents do not want to leave their home country permanently to move to the United States.) Eliseo would often tell his parents how much interest Alonzo was putting into the case, and how much he seemed to care about arresting those who put Byron and others inside the railcar. Most of all, Alonzo helped Eliseo deal with his grief during many long phone conversations.

Eliseo Acevedo and Alonzo Martinez first met in person when the government brought Eliseo to the border region of Texas that first fall to include him in an attempt to identity the smugglers. During that trip, Eliseo ended up in the same hotel as the relatives of one of the victims from Mexico. The man talked briefly with Eliseo about facing his son's death, and how hard that had been. "We both kind of patted each other on the shoulder," Eliseo recalled. He saw the same pain in the man's eyes that he saw in the eyes of his own parents.

Eliseo was later back in Texas, this time in Houston, when a federal grand jury met in the spring of 2003 to consider an indictment that was ultimately used to charge the alleged smugglers. It was the same indictment that was announced at the summer press conference in the Des Moines rail yard.

~

The investigation didn't always go as smoothly as it might have appeared to those attending the press conference. During a trip to Sarasota, Florida, in October 2002, several federal agents had a chance to talk with one of the suspected smugglers, Rogelio Hernandez. They found an apartment where they believed Rogelio was living. As they knocked and identified themselves, Rogelio slipped out the sliding glass door at the rear of the second-story apartment, jumping from the balcony. The agents had made a basic mistake of not covering the back exit. Rogelio was gone. Agents were told by those still inside the apartment that Rogelio's brother was in Florida, prepared to take Rogelio back to Mexico.

Two months later, agents were back in Sarasota to interview some people connected to the case. They also wanted to look for Rogelio, whom they believed might be in Sarasota again. As they worked their way from one interview to another, they felt they were close on the coyote's trail. The U.S. Attorney's Office in the Southern District of Texas was reluctant to have investigators make an arrest at that point, however. The attorneys didn't want to issue an arrest warrant yet because it would start the clock ticking for the speedy trial deadline, several investigators said. The Speedy Trial Act requires that trials begin within 70 days of the prosecutor filing an indictment. The attorneys wanted to be more prepared before they got things rolling.

"I remember being quite upset over that. I thought if you have the guy, you should grab him," said Estela Biesemeyer, supervisor of the Des Moines INS office. "Of course, as an investigator, what you want to do doesn't always coincide with what the U.S. Attorney wants to do, but I remember being quite upset."

More than two years would pass before agents could find Rogelio again.

The U.S. Attorney's Office in southern Texas declined to be interviewed for this book, as did the Border Patrol, citing the fact that the case officially remains open.

The anti-smuggling investigator, Gabe Bustamante, now retired from Immigration and Customs Enforcement, had his own experience with the U.S. Attorney's Office in southern Texas asking him to wait on an arrest. When the "Denison 11" investigation was in full-gear, Bustamante was helping others collect evidence against Licea, later described by the government as the ringleader. They had gotten a call from an informant who suspected that Licea had gotten a group of undocumented immigrants beyond the interior checkpoint using a train. The informant told them to watch a particular house in Kingsville. The investigators set up to watch the house from a distance. Eventually, a man walked out of a house, looked around the neighborhood and made a call from his cell phone. Within a few minutes, a car pulled up and the man with the cell phone walked out with three other people, who got into the car. The local police stopped the car soon after, confirming investigators' suspicions that the three loaded into the car were undocumented immigrants. "Once we established that, we came back and decided to hit the house knowing there was a good possibility that the Cacahuate guy [Licea] was in there," Bustamante said. "I was the one who made the decision." Bustamante made the call, setting aside the wishes of the U.S. Attorney's Office, which wanted to continue to build the case before making any arrests.

"Once you get the ball rolling, you have to be ready to move, and they were treating this thing with kid gloves ... But he was right in the middle of the group, and he was an illegal alien himself. I made the decision and it worked," Bustamante said. Licea, who had been inside the house with more than a dozen other undocumented immigrants, was temporarily taken to the holding cells at the Border Patrol checkpoint near Sarita. The investigators warned the agents there to keep a close eye on Licea.

"We put him in isolated, and the first thing he was trying to do, when a guy went to check on him, was he was trying to scratch the molding out around a window there to escape," Bustmante said.

That arrest of Licea, along with some pressure from the office of U.S. Senator Charles Grassley of Iowa, got things moving with criminal charges. Grassley's office made an inquiry on the progress of the Denison case in the aftermath of another, similar case where 19 immigrants died after being left in a sweltering trailer near Victoria, Texas.

Alonzo said he understood, as did Biesemeyer, that prosecutors necessarily look at cases from a different perspective than investigators. The attorneys are the ones who may have to present evidence in court to get a conviction. Different districts of the U.S. Attorney's Office have different styles: some are simply more cautious than others. Alonzo had worked many years with the U.S. Attorney's Office in Iowa's northern district, which had a limited role in the Denison 11 case, and with the office in Iowa's southern district. Those offices were always extremely supportive of immigration investigators' work in general over the years that Alonzo was in the Omaha office. "They supported us like I've never seen."

Alonzo has had plenty of cases where other prosecutors or his own agency wouldn't back him or others when it came to enforcing immigration-related law, however. Too often, he said, politics come into play. The one that sticks with him the most is the case in Postville, Iowa. Many Americans have heard about the "Postville Raid," or the May 2008 raid by U.S. Immigration and Customs Enforcement officials at Agriprocessors Inc. in Postville, Iowa. Few know, however, that the raid was supposed to have happened eight years earlier than it did.

When it took place, the 2008 raid on the kosher slaughterhouse and meat packing plant was the largest single workplace raid in the United States. Nearly 400 workers were arrested for using false documents. Most of the undocumented immigrants were ultimately deported back to Guatemala or other home countries after serving five-month prison sentences for document fraud. The plant closed and filed for bankruptcy, due in part to difficulties tied to the massive fraud case. The Postville City Council declared their small town a humanitarian and economic disaster area (but federal officials said the town didn't qualify for help). The former Agriprocessors facility was eventually sold, and resumed production at a lower level under a new name.

How would things have turned out if the raid had been carried out eight years earlier? The impact of the raid still would have been significant, but it's likely that as many as 200 fewer undocumented immigrants would have been arrested. Agents in 2000 had found evidence suggesting that 200-some of the workers were in the country illegally. A raid in 2000 would certainly have discouraged some of those who ultimately came from small Guatemalan villages, places heavily affected by the actual 2008 raid.

Alonzo clearly remembers the day in November 2000, when he and dozens of other agents were supposed to raid the Postville slaughterhouse. He had been waiting in Omaha all day for the go-ahead call from Washington D.C. Agents traveling from southern Texas had already gone as far as Kansas. They were to be in Iowa in a matter of hours and the group would continue to Postville in the state's northeast corner for what was certain to be a major raid. The Omaha office of the Immigration and Naturalization Service, where Alonzo worked, had done such thorough advance computer data work that the agents were almost guaranteed to arrest several hundred undocumented immigrants.

The call finally came around 4 p.m. that day. Instead of getting the go-ahead, however, Alonzo was told that the entire operation was off. It was off even though the INS had already obtained a search warrant, even though agents had already spent parts of two work days traveling from Texas and other locations, and even though all the computer work indicated that many employees at the Postville plant were not supposed to be in the United States. Alonzo was flabbergasted. They had already held off until after the presidential elections on Nov. 7, a delay that Alonzo had considered valid since a highly visible raid late in the election period could affect the outcome. It was later in November, however, and George W. Bush had already defeated Al Gore, but wouldn't take over from President Bill Clinton for a few more months.

Why was there a stand-down order? Alonzo would never be given a definitive answer, only second-hand rumors. Regardless of the reason, Alonzo was left frustrated with the feeling that his hands had been tied from doing his job as directed.

Later, during President George W. Bush's time in office, the U.S. Immigration and Customs Enforcement (ICE), the agency created in the post-9/11 years, showed a new aggressiveness in going after undocumented immigrants. Looking at statistics, the tone at ICE seemed to change around 2006. It was in that year that the United States had a significant increase in the number of arrests of undocumented immigrants, particularly through worksite raids. Before 2006, the number of arrests made at worksites annually was typically around 500. The numbers subsequently began to climb as large-scale immigration raids became more commonplace. ICE reported 1,116 "administrative" worksite enforcement arrests in 2005. By the following year, that number had jumped to 3,667, an increase of 229 percent. The arrests climbed to 5,184 by 2008.

The increase in worksite arrests was a big piece of an overall increase in all "removals" by ICE during that period. In fiscal year

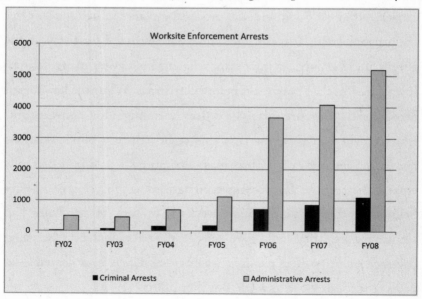

Source: U.S. Immigration and Customs Enforcement

2002, just over 116,000 undocumented immigrants were removed from the United States. The numbers climbed steadily to just over 349,000 in 2008.

While many applauded this level of enforcement, it seemed to leave a sour taste in the mouths of other, previously uninterested Americans. Some didn't feel quite right watching uniformed ICE agents raid the plant down the road, or watching people who had become part of their community led out in handcuffs. As worksite raids became more common, protests began to follow. It became almost a certainty that relatives, friends, and sympathetic neighbors of those taken into custody would demonstrate in the days immediately following a major raid. Those demonstrations didn't always continue beyond the first week, but they did send a message that at least one segment of the population wasn't happy that ICE was enforcing the law this way. But immigration officials, for whatever reason, seemed to be pandering less to Americans' sensitivities.

On December 12, 2006, for example, immigration raids were carried out at six Swift and Co. processing plants in five states. Over 1,200 people were arrested. December 12th was the feast day of the Virgin of Guadalupe, an important religious holiday for many Latinos. It was also less than two weeks before Christmas. While the law doesn't take a holiday at Christmas, the bosses at Immigration and Customs Enforcement had to know that this could create a public-relations headache. The upcoming Christmas celebrations would have certainly crossed their minds. The bosses would have known that they could have held off on the raids a few more weeks or months and probably had similar results. They could have avoided the television and newspaper coverage of teary-eyed relatives waiting—as Christmas neared—for news of those arrested at work. But they didn't.

Did someone give the go-ahead to aggressively enforce the nation's laws at this time to purposely stir things up? It was as if the intent was to say, "Okay, you want us to enforce the law exactly as it's written? Here we go." Could this have been a deliberate attempt on the part of the government to bring the issue of immigration to the forefront? During this time, then-President Bush was working hard for comprehensive immigration reform. He needed the public behind him if Congress were to back him. Perhaps the White House or ICE administrators decided that the best thing that could have happened was that Americans started paying more attention to the issue. Aggressively enforcing the current law—as distasteful as some people found it—may have been viewed as the best route to new law. Was it the only way to get people to care about reform?

Or, perhaps, it was more straight-forward than that. ICE officials may have grown tired of hearing complaints about how the current laws were not being enforced. They simply decided to set aside considerations such as disruptions to holidays and the resulting mood of the American people as they aggressively enforced the law.

If there was no intention to send a message to the American people, did ICE simply decide it had to do more to justify to Congress the manpower and money it was receiving in the post-9/11 years? The organization needed to show its effectiveness and worksite arrests were a quick way to achieve that. At the same time, it sent a message to businesses to stop hiring undocumented workers. ICE didn't downplay its stepped-up enforcement. Its annual reports in those years addressed the drive to send home more undocumented immigrants. An October 23, 2008, press release from ICE stated:

"Reflecting the impact of heightened, strategic enforcement efforts, U.S. Immigration and Customs

Enforcement (ICE) efforts reached record levels in virtually every enforcement category in fiscal year 2008, from criminal, gang and fugitive alien arrests to federal prosecutions and formal deportations. The significant increase is a direct result of ICE's expanded interior immigration enforcement strategy, focusing on three priorities—targeting criminal and fugitive aliens; eliminating the magnet of illegal employment; and dismantling the infrastructure that supports illegal immigration including the criminal organizations engaged in wide-spread identity theft and document fraud."

If Alonzo Martinez had still been doing immigration investigations for the government out of Omaha, he likely would have been part of the later raid, in 2008. This time, there was no stand-down call. It was late spring 2008 and the last half-year of President George W. Bush's final term. Immigration and Customs Enforcement agents descended on Postville and arrested nearly one-third of the workforce at Agriprocessors Inc., then the largest kosher slaughterhouse in the United States. In a small town like Postville, Iowa, then with an estimated population of 2,800, this is not the kind of thing that would slip by with little notice. The town was in an uproar. Demonstrations began almost immediately. The local Catholic Church and others in town did what they could to help the families of those arrested. They spoke to the media on behalf of the families. The schools paid extra attention to the needs of children of the arrested workers.

Regardless of the reasons or motivations, the result of more removals by ICE appeared to be an increased interest in the topic of immigration. The new aggressiveness lit fires that were not lit before.

Immigrants appeared to demonstrate on a larger scale—although perhaps still only occasionally—in the immediate aftermaths of large-scale raids. Americans who didn't pay much attention before sat up and took notice.

At the same time, another group of Americans applauded ICE for its attempt to follow the letter of the law. This well-organized segment of the population had been frustrated with what they felt was lazy enforcement on the part of the government. They continued to speak up against guest worker or amnesty programs, to applaud the increase in removals and to demand more.

The same year that ICE statistics began to show a big increase in removals, Gallup found a jump in the percentage of Americans who thought immigration was the most important problem facing the United States. Almost two in ten Americans surveyed ranked immigration as the top issue. Immigration also landed among the top five issues of concern for the first time since Gallup began tracking. The increased interest in immigration, however, didn't bring about any dramatic change. President Bush failed to get Congress on board for comprehensive immigration reform in 2006 and 2007, perhaps because those opposed to relaxing immigration policy were most effective in getting their message across. Over the next year, the nation geared up for the 2008 presidential election, and Americans continued to show widespread interest. In mid-2007, 15 percent of those polled by the *Los Angeles Times*/Bloomberg said illegal immigration was *the* number one issue on their minds when deciding which candidate to back. If this polling data were extrapolated to the entire U.S. population, we'd be talking about some 30 million adults who had immigration on their minds more than any other political topic. Another 66 percent said it was not their top issue, but was still an important one as they decided how to vote.

In the earliest stages of the primary season, immigration received a lot of attention. Some of the individuals competing for their party's nomination ran television commercials focusing solely on immigration. In the final months of the campaign, however, as Senator John McCain and Senator Barack Obama were facing off one-on-one, the issue took a back seat to the worsening economy and energy concerns. Perhaps both men were being cautious by avoiding a topic that had created such a rift in the population. The word "immigration" came up only once— and only in context of another discussion—in the three presidential debates. Even though the presidential candidates were not talking about it much, immigration reform was on their to-do lists. It was part of their platforms. Obama and McCain both promised comprehensive reform, and their plans on getting there were similar. They wanted to allow undocumented immigrants to become legal residents by meeting certain conditions. But there was an added emphasis on security, especially by McCain, who had otherwise been known for bucking his party's platform on immigration. McCain promised to finish the fence along the U.S.-Mexican border and step up enforcement. Presumably, this was an attempt to appease Americans who were still focused on tougher enforcement, while dangling the hope of future change before others.

The election of President Barack Obama and the shift of power toward the Democrats in Congress seemed—to media pundits—to signal a greater likelihood of major change. As of the publishing of this book, however, that change had not materialized. Obama has said immigration reform is still on his to-do list, but many, including some who voted for him on this platform, grew restless after his first 100-days—and then two years—passed with no significant change.

Syndicated columnist Ruben Navarrette Jr. wrote in 2008 that the Democrats have immigration reform as a low priority because of organized labor. "Democrats' slavish adherence to unions require that they derail any proposal that includes guest workers, as any bill with a chance to win Republican support would have to do," Navarrette wrote.

Tom Barry, then writing for the Center for International Policy, summarized the situation like this shortly after Obama was elected:

"On the night of his victory, President-elect Obama told Americans and the world that his electoral triumph demonstrated that 'all things are possible' in America. But comprehensive immigration reform is one of the things that just may not be possible given the rabid opposition of grassroots restrictionists, the still-sizable Republican opposition, the strength of 'moderate' Democrats, and the lack of political will among liberal Democrats. Not during the campaign or in his short career in the Senate has comprehensive immigration reform been a priority for Obama, and it likely won't be a priority as president, despite a July [2008] promise at the National Council of La Raza convention to tackle the issue."

Will those Americans who haven't liked how the law looks when it's aggressively enforced be heard over those who object to major immigration reform? Obama will not be let off the hook easily on his election-year promise of change, even if there's some inertia to overcome in Congress. The world of immigration is not a stagnant pool. Even when it's not glaringly obvious, a troublesome current runs under the surface. Americans are clearly dissatisfied with the current system but are at odds over which direction to go.

Chapter Fourteen

It was June 2005, three years after the group of eleven climbed inside the grain hopper. The sky was beginning to grow light as dawn arrived in the central Mexican state of Aguascalientes. Mexican authorities moved in to a neighborhood near the city of Aguascalientes, and arrested Rogelio Hernandez Ramos, one of the three main smugglers charged in connection with the deaths of the eleven.

Rogelio's arrest was covered by the Mexican newspaper *El Universal*. The newspaper's reporter talked with relatives of Omar Esparza Contreras and Roberto Esparza Rico, the two victims from the state of Aguascalientes. The parents of the two had become more resigned about the deaths in the past few years, but weren't yet ready to forgive the coyote. "We cannot pardon that person, and ... although it is not going to give back to us our children, we want and we know that he is going to pay for his sins," Juvenal Esparza Rico, Omar's father, told *El Universal*.

Two and a half years had passed since members of the U.S. task force investigating the deaths wanted to arrest Rogelio in Florida. During the intervening years, U.S. authorities had been unable to nab Rogelio, accused of smuggling the two Mexicans.

On that June morning in 2005, however, he was arrested in Mexico, where he remained in prison as of mid-2010. Rogelio's arrest in Mexico did not resolve the charges he was facing in the United States, however. He was still a wanted man north of the border, but U.S. authorities were unable to get him extradited to the United States at the time of his arrest. Mexican officials don't have to hand over wanted suspects to the United States when the person is accused of a crime that is punishable by death. The charges against Rogelio included conspiring to smuggle undocumented workers for personal gain where a death resulted. This is a crime punishable by death. Under a treaty addressing such extradition attempts, Mexico is supposed to hand over a suspect if U.S. authorities give assurances that the government will not seek or impose the death penalty, even though it would be an option. Mexico has decided it would like this assurance to come from a judge rather than a prosecutor, but this judicial assurance is not a valid possibility since a U.S. judge can't rule on something not officially before him or her.

In public, prosecutors did not initially rule out the possibility of the death penalty or life imprisonment—another penalty frowned upon by Mexican officials—for Rogelio's case, which would have made Mexican officials reluctant to cooperate. By 2004, however, prosecutors wrote in court documents that they would not seek the death penalty in regard to the case of another smuggler, Licea.

The United States may again try to extradite Rogelio, particularly once his scheduled release in Mexico nears.

Licea, the government-described ringleader, had been arrested years earlier, in 2003, when Gabe Bustamante, a member of the Border Patrol's anti-smuggling unit, made the call to move in on a stash house. Licea, who government officials say was involved in smuggling people for almost five years, later entered a guilty plea to one count under a plea agreement that included the dropping of other charges. He was sentenced in November 2005 to more than 24 years in prison for his role in the smuggling operation that resulted in deaths.

Licea and his various attorneys have made attempts to overturn his conviction. He initially argued that he didn't understand that he was admitting responsibility for the eleven deaths as a result of the plea agreement. He said he believed he was simply admitting involvement in a smuggling operation. "I have always told them and I have affirmed that I am not responsible for having put those people on the train," Licea told a judge during his sentencing hearing. He then argued that his guides, or those working with other smugglers, had carried out the actual placement of the individuals in that specific train. He and the judge had the following conversation:

Judge: "Didn't you get the train schedules?"

Licea: "Yes, but not in this case."

Judge: "Didn't you get the scheduling?"

Licea: "Yes."

Judge: "And didn't you make arrangements, either yourself or through other people—according to your own plea—didn't you make those arrangements with your own people to schedule people to get on not necessarily that train, but on trains period?"

Licea: "Yes, but when I did that, there was no accident or nothing bad happened."

Judge: "Well, I'm not saying something bad did happen on other occasions, but you had made arrangements with a person to get the train schedules and you supplied information and you collected the money for even these people who were on that train, didn't you?"

Licea's attorney then took over the conversation, explaining that Licea and Flores, the conductor, may have had a falling out around this time and may not have been speaking directly around the time the eleven were loaded. Legally, it didn't seem to matter. Licea has, so far, had little luck with his various legal maneuvers in the court system. Licea did, however, convince the State Bar of Texas disciplinary counsel that another attorney he hired in 2007 had been negligent in his responsibilities toward Licea. The attorney ultimately agreed to make payments to Licea as part of a partial refund of a $10,000 retainer fee that had been paid to the attorney by Licea's relatives. The attorney has since filed for bankruptcy.

The former Union Pacific conductor, Arnulfo Flores, Jr., has already served his time in prison. He received a lighter sentence for conspiring to smuggle the undocumented immigrants because of his cooperation with investigators. He was arrested in 2003, and released about three years later.

"It seemed like the world was coming to an end," Flores said of that day he got a call from Alonzo Martinez, who asked Flores to come talk to him at an immigration office building in Harlingen. "Everything that we [Flores and his wife] had worked for was gone pretty much and there was nothing I could do about it. At that point in time, I had already come to terms with it and had already told my wife that I was going to face whatever was there."

Flores described his years in prison as the longest of his life. His family stood behind him, however, which helped. His wife was there to visit almost every time she had a chance. Flores is now trying to rebuild his life. As of 2010, he was working for a company doing concrete construction work. He was in charge of making sure the concrete quality was what it should be. Ironically, the man who once made money helping slip undocumented immigrants into the country would now, as part of his construction job, help build a portion of the border wall designed to keep undocumented immigrants out. He agreed to talk about this case because of his desire to make sure his teen-age son fully understood what happened. And, perhaps, it was a bit of penance for the deaths, although he insists he does not feel responsible, just sorry for the families.

Several others involved that night as guides or assistants were charged through other, unrelated smuggling cases.

Alonzo Martinez, who spent months on the case, outlines the line of responsibility this way:

> "First and foremost are the aliens themselves. They willfully climbed in into those hoppers because they had a destination. But even more responsible are the smugglers, the coyotes. This is their business. A person is nothing more than just a piece of meat. They are cargo, they are merchandise. They will take their money and they will put them in whatever mode is available to them, usually the cheapest and the most expeditious."

As for Eliseo Acevedo, it frustrates him that none of those charged seem to feel any responsibility for his little brother's death.

"I think the train conductor is the worst because he knew they were there," Eliseo said. "I don't care what he says right now—that he wasn't involved, that he only gave them the schedules … he could have just opened the door for them or called immigration and saved their lives. So I personally think he's just as responsible as the smugglers, but they give him, what, four or five years? You kill a dog intentionally, I think they give more time than that."

With Flores having served his sentence, Licea behind bars in the United States, and Rogelio in jail in Mexico, Eliseo Acevedo still can't put his brother's death behind him. Guillermo Madrigal Ballesteros, believed to be the one who made arrangements with Byron to travel through Mexico and into Texas, has never been arrested. Alonzo suspects the man, also known as "Don Memo," has fled to Guatemala, Byron's own home country, or another Central American country where he could essentially disappear.

Shortly after the bodies were found in Iowa, Eliseo received a phone call from Madrigal.

"He wanted to know if the people that were found in Iowa were their people," Eliseo said. "And I said, 'Yes.' And he goes to me: 'We kind of knew that that was what happened, but we couldn't really say anything. And I just wanted to make sure it was them.' And I said, 'Yeah, it was them.'

"And he says to me, 'I don't know what to tell you but'—using a bad word—he says, 'those things happen' like he didn't really care. He was the coldest person I ever talked to when it comes to knowing that they killed eleven people and they didn't even blink an eye to do it."

Eliseo wants Madrigal found, and Rogelio brought to the United States to answer to the charges here.

"The smugglers knew exactly where they put them," Eliseo Acevedo said. "The train conductor knew exactly where they were. They just cleaned their hands up and said they didn't know about it .... They could have made an anonymous call and said there are eleven people in so and so car, get them out. And they left them to die in there like if they were animals. So they could have saved their lives. They didn't care. Those people only care for their money, whether they make it or not, and that's it."

~

Byron Acevedo's body now rests in Guatemala. His name is etched into the stone that stands at his burial spot. His late brother, Carlos, is next to him. Their mother treats the place like a shrine. It is a place she goes to remember the boys she lost, to pay her respects over and over, and to try to find peace.

Eliseo will never forget the day he brought Byron's body home to his mother. He still becomes emotional when he talks about it. He flew Byron's body back to Guatemala on a commercial flight. Eliseo sat in a regular passenger seat. His little brother came home in a steel box below, in the plane's cargo hold. It was what Eliseo considers the worst moment in his life.

Arriving in Guatemala was no better.

"Seeing my brother come out on a forklift in a box was painful, something that I don't wish on anybody to go through that," he said. "And I had to go through the pain, and bring him to my mom like that."

Eliseo Acevedo and Alonzo Martinez both find themselves wondering at times about those final hours. While they now know that Byron and the others likely died within a day or so of climbing into the train, they continue to dwell on it at times. And the unlikely friends occasionally trade calls or send cards around the holidays, both haunted by the absence of an ambitious Guatemalan farm boy who wanted to be like his big brother.

"He was probably one of the more focused on trying to do what I did," Eliseo said. "I think that he would have made it. He was a very clean kid, very good with people, good with everybody. And he would have made it."

Lately, Eliseo has been thinking he might have an answer to finally put his little brother to rest. He wants to get on a plane to Des Moines, and catch a cab across the city to the east side. He would like to meet someone with Union Pacific or with the U.S. Attorney's Office at the rail yard, and be led along rows and rows of track to the now-rusting railcar that was his brother's tomb for four months.

The blue grain hopper still sat at the Des Moines rail yard as of summer 2010, protected and saved as potential evidence in a criminal case that has yet to be closed. "It'll be sitting here when I die, and it'll be sitting here when you die," said one Des Moines rail yard worker, apparently skeptical that the case will ever be officially closed.

If Eliseo makes the visit to Des Moines, he wants to look inside the railcar. It's a visit that his friend Alonzo Martinez thinks would be a mistake. It is not the kind of the place that Alonzo thinks would bring about a satisfactory moment of closure for Eliseo. Still, Eliseo, a determined man, would likely peer through the hole cut by Des Moines firefighters years earlier. He would recall what he knows about Byron's final days.

He believes he needs this.

"It's kind of like a personal thing to help me to go through all of this," Eliseo said. "It's been years, and I still am hoping to see that train."

So many years ago, Eliseo was able to ease the poverty and struggles that his parents and siblings faced. He did it through hard work and determination. In a sense, he saved his family. He is still trying to come to grips with the fact that he couldn't save Byron or his two other deceased siblings. He understands that perhaps it was the money that he first used to help save his family that also later tempted Byron, in part, to leave behind his comfortable life in Guatemala.

It is a painful twist for a man dwelling so much on a train that went nowhere.

Chapter Fifteen

Epilogue

Friends and acquaintances would ask B.J. Schany what it was like to find the bodies. Did it shake him up? Did he have to be treated by a professional? Did he go into denial about what he had seen?

If Schany chose to speak frankly, he would tell them that none of that happened. Although he was stunned to find bodies during an otherwise routine work day, he didn't dwell on it nor need the help of a professional. First, there were distractions. His pregnant wife called within an hour of Schany discovering the bodies. Schany hadn't even had the chance to tell her yet what had happened when she called because she was having contractions. She met him at work. He had left to take her to an Omaha hospital by the time most of the federal investigators arrived. In the end, the contractions turned out to be false, and their daughter waited about a month longer, arriving safely. He was too worried about his unborn daughter and his wife, Jill, who was his high school sweetheart, to dwell on what had happened. Jill Schany remembers talking about the bodies during the drive to Omaha. "He didn't seem shaken up. Obviously, yeah, he was shocked, but later on he made the comment that it would have been different if they were more 'real' looking," Jill Schany said.

It is the flesh that ties us to the humanity of a body; the curve of a cheek, the shape of a nose, the turn of a mouth. When a body is reduced to bones, it becomes more remote. For all of us except professionals, the visual clues that a body might belong, for example, to a Guatemalan man who was barely more than a boy disappear with the flesh. Schany felt that distance. "I'm not a blood and guts guy, but they looked like skeletons," he said. "I felt bad for the families and stuff, but I guess I didn't have any side effects. To this day, that's the number one thing people ask me."

B.J. Schany and his wife, who have long since moved their young family from Denison back to their hometown in northern Iowa, say B.J. is also just an easy-going guy who reacts to crisis in a measured way. "I did think about what it was like for them inside a lot, and about how terrible it must be to put yourself in that circumstance," he said. "I've been low in my life, but never to a point where you'd take somebody's word to let them be locked in there." Through it all, B.J. Schany tried to be considerate when he was asked questions about the bodies. "I didn't want to make a big deal out of it. I was trying to respect the families."

❧

Some of the families still keep in touch with Alonzo Martinez, the retired INS supervisor, though the contact has grown more sporadic as time passes. Alonzo is a restless retiree. He is happiest working, and has taken a variety of jobs to keep himself busy since leaving immigration work. For a while, he worked for a contractor helping arrange the transportation needed to return undocumented immigrants to their home countries. Later, he took a job delivering mail for the U.S. Postal Service. He keeps a donkey on his rural Texas property, and is happiest when he's outdoors. He felt toward the end of his time with immigration that his supervisors believed he was dedicating too much time and energy toward the "Denison 11" case. There were other fish to fry, and he was encouraged to focus on other cases. Those still wanted may eventually wind up in a U.S. courtroom. Alonzo knew he had to accept this, and let the case go.

His friend, Eliseo Acevedo, struggled to accept that some of those charged have not yet answered for their role in his little brother's death. Some of his family feels the same way. Eliseo's mother still makes frequent visits to the graves of her children. The family couldn't stand to sell Byron's horse, Muchacho, though no one rides much anymore. It wanders the hills around the farm, thinner now without Byron irrigating the hills when rain is scarce.

In November 2010, Eliseo had to make a trip from his New York home to Omaha. Instead of jumping on a plane to return to New York after his business was done, he rented a car and headed east to Des Moines. He knew that the railcar where Byron died still sat somewhere in a Union Pacific rail yard in Des Moines, preserved as possible evidence in a future trial. He had to try to see it, and didn't know when he'd be this close again. He arrived in Des Moines late one evening and grabbed a hotel room. The next morning, he wound his way around the east side of Des Moines, eventually finding the Union Pacific yard. Driving toward it, he knew he may have come all this way only to be turned away. He dreaded that, desperate for a step he felt might bring him closure.

Instead, against all odds, he was given that chance. Eliseo crossed numerous tracks, and, without hesitation, walked up to GVSR 518018. The opening cut into the side had long since been closed again, brackets welded on to reattach the piece that had been cut out. Rust now rimmed the rectangle. Against the backdrop of a noisy rail yard, he placed his hand against the cold side. A small hole remained where the welder had been unable to make a perfect seal. Eliseo peeked inside, seeing a dark bottom space that seemed impossibly small for eleven people. This was the place where Byron had died.

Eliseo walked to the railcar's end, looking for the ladder Byron would have climbed to reach the top. At the opposite end, he paused, struggling alone with his emotions for a moment as an unseasonably warm wind whipped through the yard. He stared at the top of the railcar, remembering what he knew of a June day so long ago. His head dropped.

Eliseo didn't linger for long.

His wife and sons were waiting for him in New York.

It was time to get back to the living.

Eliseo Acevedo's November 2010 visit to railcar.

Acknowledgments

I am grateful my husband, Darin, who set aside his doubts about this project fitting into our lives to help me find time to write. I forget to say it sometimes in the midst of raising small children, but I know how much your choices make mine possible. Thanks also to my children—Logan, Luke, and Paige, who were good sports about having less of my time and attention during the past half year. Your curiosity about the world reminds me to hold on to my own. To my mom, Mary Bradford, who repeatedly and enthusiastically offered to watch my kids, perhaps the biggest factor in my getting this written. Your editing help was also invaluable. She and my dad, Jim Bradford, taught me to love books, writing, and learning, a big factor in my career choice. Thanks to my siblings and in-laws, who were also supportive in so many ways. Many friends encouraged me, watched my children, proof-read portions of the book, or helped in other ways. I can't list them all, but they include: Gabriela Finnegan, Tricia Garton, Marty Helle, Mei-Ling Hopgood, Brandi Christian-Judkins, Jodi Kuhse, Jennifer Dukes Lee, John Moore, John Mullen, Tom O'Donnell, Monte Reel, Kristina Sauerwein, Jeff Snyder, Christine Thompson, Becky Waller, and Jennifer Wilson. My gratitude to Mike McNarney, whose editing suggestions were a great help. A special thanks to Storytellers International President, Paul Kakert, director of our companion documentary, for his enthusiasm for this story from the moment he heard about it. He and graphics artist Vijaya Raghavan were kind enough to provide many of the photos and graphics seen in this book. I'm grateful to Wayne Bruns from Iowa Public Television who encouraged me to tell this story on television at a point when I might have set it aside entirely. Dawn Frederick, my literary agent from Red Sofa Literary Agency, was confident in this book's chances from the start. Thanks to her for her world-class guidance and editing. I am particularly grateful to my publisher, Steve Semken of Ice Cube Press, for seeing the potential in this project and deciding to help me get it on the shelves. Finally, thanks to the families of the eleven and the investigators for sharing their stories.

Colleen Bradford Krantz graduated from Iowa State University with a degree in journalism. After graduating, she reported for the *St. Louis Post-Dispatch*'s metro desk. She then worked as a *Milwaukee Journal Sentinel* reporter, before eventually becoming a state desk reporter for *The Des Moines Register*. Now an independent journalist, Colleen has written and co-produced her first documentary, *Train to Nowhere; Inside an Immigrant Death Investigation*. This book, the starting point for the documentary, is her first. She lives near Adel, Iowa, with her husband and three children. For more information on Colleen go to www.ColleenBradfordKrantz.com.

The companion documentary, *Train to Nowhere; Inside an Immigrant Death Investigation,* offers an honest, yet compassionate look at the 2002 railcar deaths of the eleven undocumented immigrants. The film, which first broadcast in the fall of 2010 on a PBS affiliate, is part crime story, part immigration perspective. One online reviewer wrote for www.AllVoices.com: "The emotionally charged national controversy over immigration takes an uncharacteristically calm position in the new documentary film... *Train to Nowhere's* tone is consistently nonjudgmental. Each player in the investigation is interviewed, and they all get a fair hearing..." Colleen Bradford Krantz was writer and co-producer of the documentary. Paul Kakert of Storytellers International was director and co-producer. The DVD is available at www.TrainToNowhere.com

Ice Cube Books began publishing in 1993 to focus on how to live with the natural world and to better understand how people can best live together in the communities they share and inhabit. Since this time, we've been recognized by a number of well-known writers, including Gary Snyder, Gene Logsdon, Wes Jackson, Patricia Hampl, Greg Brown, Maxine Kumin, Jim Harrison, Annie Dillard, Ken Burns, Kathleen Norris, Janisse Ray, Alison Deming, Richard Rhodes, Michael Pollan, and Barry Lopez. We've published a number of well-known authors as well, including Mary Swander, Jim Heynen, Mary Pipher, Bill Holm, Connie Mutel, John T. Price, Carol Bly, Marvin Bell, Debra Marquart, Ted Kooser, Stephanie Mills, Bill McKibben, and Paul Gruchow. As well, we have won several publishing awards over the last seventeen years. Check out our books at our web site, with booksellers, or at museum shops, then discover why we strive to "hear the other side."

Ice Cube Press (est. 1993)
205 N Front Street
North Liberty, Iowa 52317-9302
steve@icecubepress.com
www.icecubepress.com

across, over, around, and
down every type of track
to my co-horts aboard this
never-ending adventure
Fenna Marie & Laura Lee

ENVIRONMENTAL BENEFITS STATEMENT

Ice Cube Press saved the following resources by printing the pages of this book on chlorine free paper made with 100% post-consumer waste.

TREES	WATER	SOLID WASTE	GREENHOUSE GASES
6	**2,725**	**165**	**566**
FULLY GROWN	GALLONS	POUNDS	POUNDS

Calculations based on research by Environmental Defense and the Paper Task Force. Manufactured at Friesens Corporation